ART SUBLIMATION OR SYMPTOM

CONTEMPORARY THEORY SERIES

Series Editor: Frances Restuccia, Professor of English, Boston College

ART
SUBLIMATION OR SYMPTOM

EDITED BY
PARVEEN ADAMS

KARNAC
LONDON   NEW YORK

Permission to reprint the following is gratefully acknowledged:

Stills from Alfred Hitchcock's *Vertigo* © 2003 by Universal Studios, Courtesy of Universal Studios Publishing Rights, a Division of Universal Studies Licensing, Inc. All rights reserved.

The Lute Player, Caravaggio (1573-1610) and *Victorious Cupid*, Caravaggio, courtesy of Nimatallah/Art Resource, N.Y.; *The Sacrifice of Isaac*, Caravaggio (1603-1604), courtesy of Scala/Art Resources, N.Y.; *Lincoln Conspirator Lewis Payne*, courtesy of the Boston Public Library, Print Department. Photograph by Alexander Gardner, 1865.

Las Meninas, New Mexico, 1987; Leda, Los Angeles, 1986; Feast of Fools, Mexico City, 1990; and the Guernica Variations, New Mexico, 1986, courtesy of Fraenkel Gallery, San Francisco.

Graham Hamill's essay is adapted from chapter 3 of his book, *Sexuality and Form*. Copyright 2000 by The University of Chicago. All rights reserved.

Production Editor: Robert D. Hack
This book was set in 11 pt Berkeley by Alpha Graphics of Pittsfield, NH.

Published in UK 2003 by
H. Karnac (Books) Ltd,
118 Finchley Road,
London NW3 5HT

ISBN: 978 1 85575 914 5

Published in US by Other Press LLC.

www.karnacbooks.com

Printed and bound in Great Britain by Berforts Information Press Ltd.

for my mother, Gul, and my father, Jal

Contents

Foreword

We are delighted to include Parveen Adams' *Art: Sublimation or Symptom* in the Contemporary Theory series at Other Press. *Art* is a varied collection whose essays bear Adams' stamp of distinction. She has a keen eye for what is fascinating and radically new, and this collection will enhance its readers' sense of that gift. Another gift is also on display here: her ability to join psychoanalysis and art for productive purposes. Adams knows what concept to fit with what work of art. She writes frankly that "writings on psychoanalysis and art have always been disappointing." But, as she implicitly promises, the essays in her collection are anything but bland.

More specifically, this study breathes fresh life into the concept of sublimation. It is here rescued from its dull duty of channeling sexual energy into acceptable cultural forms. What is emphasized is that aspect of the concept of sublimation that takes it beyond the pleasure principle, as an index of the Real. The *sinthome* of course also concerns the Real, but quite differently. Adams thus sustains the current wave of interest in Lacan's concept of the *sinthome* that links the three rings (Imaginary, Symbolic, and Real) of the Borromean knot.

In some respects, then, *Art: Sublimation or Symptom* serves as a companion piece to Luke Thurston's collection, *Re-inventing the Symptom,* also in this series. Together, they stretch Lacanian theory to its limits. Adams is, in fact, a brilliant theorist in her own right. She imports Lacan into domains he could not have dreamed he would end up in. She teases out every implication of his theory.

For those readers unschooled in the nuances of Lacanian theory, *Art: Sublimation or Symptom* includes essays that offer some training. I have supplemented my own teaching of Lacan with the lucid, methodical, and instructive essays by Franz Kaltenbeck and Geneviève Morel. Adams' collection teaches its reader about Lacan and, in particular, late Lacan. And—though the point is the imbrication of the two realms—it equally gives the reader tools for accessing art, for knowing how to zero in on what is critical about a novel: Luke Thurston engages Schlink's *The Reader*; film—Mark Cousins analyzes Hitchcock's *Vertigo*; painting—Graham Hammill psychoanalytically queers Caravaggio's masterpieces; and photographic theory—Juli Carson reads Barthes' *Camera Lucida* as itself an instance of psychical work. These essays also draw from non-Lacanian theorists—Adorno, Derrida, Blanchot, Bersani, Sedgwick—who give this study an intellectual breadth, further projecting it beyond Lacan.

While it would be an understatement to assert that the Contemporary Theory series is friendly to Lacan, it is by no means solely dedicated to Lacanian studies. We are looking for smart, new theoretical work with important practical consequences, work that transgresses the limits of theory as it now stands and exposes the necessary overlap of theory with the world in which we live, day by day. This series welcomes all theory being done currently in, for example, feminist, queer, and other political contexts, film studies, or aesthetics—even theoretically inclined novels are invited. *Art: Sublimation or Symptom* itself has been written for a heterogeneous audience: art historians, art critics, artists, film theorists, psychoanalytic theorists, psychoanalysts, and students of contemporary theory in general.

Frances L. Restuccia
Series Editor

Preface: Way beyond the Pleasure Principle

PARVEEN ADAMS

Writings on psychoanalysis and art have always been disappointing. It is as though the fusion of two such febrile topics has resulted in an unexpected blandness. Psychoanalysis, when used to explain art, becomes timid. It conceives of art in terms of a creativity where imaginary forms constitute an alternative expression of the artist's sexual drive. The work of art merely seems to invite a naïve psychology of the artist. For this reason, the category that had seemed to broker the arranged marriage—sublimation—has rightly attracted hostility. But sublimation as the satisfaction of the drive is a problematic metapsychological concept that is no simple thing and that turns out to be intimately linked with the death drive. For those for whom sublimation seems a suspect regression within Freudian thought, one that enables the psychical conditions of art production to be represented in a respectable, desexualized form, this volume constitutes an unorthodox presentation of the complexity and unresolved character of the Freudian position. Certainly Lacan, whose own development of the theory of sublimation was integral to his work, was untroubled by any suspicion of subjective idealism in the Freudian conception of sublimation. For Lacan the real issue of sublimation concerns not the humanist problem of creativity but the problem of a creation *ex nihilo*, and he relates to the Freudian metapsychology through the category of the Real.

There is no single theory of sublimation in Freud but rather a number of loosely woven strands developed to varying degrees. Nonetheless the theory of sublimation is from the first about the satisfaction of the drive. But where Freud indicated a change in the sexual aim of the drive, Lacan's theory of sublimation involved a change in the nature of the object toward which the drive is directed. In the seminar on ethics he writes, "An object, insofar as it is a created object, may fill the function that enables it not to avoid the Thing as signifier, but to represent it." For Lacan sublimation enables the object to index the Thing. It is not the aim of this volume to document the details of these theories and the problems associated with them. Nor is it the aim of this Preface to preempt the contributions to this volume. Three points concerning sublimation should suffice here: (1) the idea of the satisfaction of the drive (though this may be accounted for in different ways); (2) the social nature of sublimation that is insisted on by both Freud and Lacan; and (3) the link between sublimation and ethics that Lacan made in his seminar on ethics. These are the issues taken up in various ways by many of the contributors to this volume.

Others are not concerned with sublimation but write instead about a second and quite different theory of creation that Lacan invented in his late seminar on James Joyce, *Le Sinthome*. There the place of the symptom (*sinthome*) is crucial. This book explores both the theory of sublimation and the theory of the *sinthome*. The difference between them is a question of the status of *jouissance*. It could be said that while sublimation touches on the Real, the *sinthome* partakes of the Real.

The aim of this book, however, goes beyond the exegesis of theory. It should be noted that much current psychoanalytic work on art fails to engage with the art object and restricts itself essentially to treating it as an exemplification or the instantiation of a theoretical point. Lacan himself can be reproached for raiding the art work for a certain subjective register of the artist that is then, in an unmediated fashion, carried back into the psychoanalytic theory of the subject. Psychoanalysis has often a faux-modest attitude toward art, expressed in the formula, "Art has much to teach psychoanalysis; psychoanalysis has very little to say to art." The apparent modesty of this formula conceals a certain theoretical arrogance—the transaction between the two has increased the power of psychoanalysis but not that of art. Perhaps it would be truer to say, "Art has much to teach psychoanalysis about art" and "Psychoanalysis has much to teach art about psychoanalysis." The question is not who teaches whom but their mutual capacity to stay together long enough for something to happen.

Contributors to the volume move between text and psychoanalytic theory without privileging the one over the other. Here something does happen. For our concern is to analyze the picture or novel *itself* rather than the artist or the author. And this process engenders a development of psychoanalytic theory. This is not surprising, since we begin with the conviction that pictures, written texts, and filmic texts operate in a psychical space. The meeting with psychoanalytic theory does not require that a violence be done to either theory or text.

This volume, then, is not concerned with consolidating the idea of sublimation either in Freud or in Lacan. The strength of these ideas is tested here, not through a set of logical criteria for theoretical excellence but, instead, through their productiveness. What can this or that aspect of the theory bring to the analysis of cultural objects? And to what extent do these objects themselves provide a spur to the inflection or rearticulation of theory?

Mark Cousins' essay does not address the issue of sublimation directly. In Lacan's terms, sublimation is the raising of the object to the dignity of the Thing, that which is outside representation. The essay approaches this idea through the analysis of the *image*, in particular, Hitchcock's *Vertigo* and the problem of the relation between images and their objects. He uses Hitchcock and the film to provide a brisk critique of a type of psychoanalytic criticism that is to be found in much film theory that stresses oedipal identifications and the link between images and unconscious objects. The image that captivates Scottie is not an image of someone, of an object; the image plays a distinct and autonomous role—it is always already an "image of loss" and not the image of a lost object. In the second half of the film, the hero works to reconstruct an image, not to recover an object. Paradoxically the perfection of the image causes the breakdown of the scene. Judy is forced to increasingly take on the image that was once Madeleine's. Finally there is an anamorphotic moment: the sight of Judy, the image of Madeleine wearing the jewels of Carlotta Valdes. It is a moment of impossible perfection that finally disengages Scottie from the image. The question that the essay leaves unresolved from the point of view of sublimation is whether the process Mark Cousins describes is a kind of resistance to sublimation or whether it should be regarded as a part of it.

Luke Thurston contrasts Freud's idea of sublimation as read by Adorno with Lacan's idea of sublimation as developed in the ethics seminar. The shift is from some kind of model of the pacification of the drive to one where the drive's disruption of meaning is brought to the fore. For Adorno the Holocaust was "incommensurable with experience as such" and hence something that cannot be made meaningful. The link with Lacan is the relation to the unrepresentable in sublimation. Lacan makes the point through the idea of anamorphosis, which explains how something can be incompatible with our normal way of seeing. What makes Lacan even more pertinent is sublimation's link with ethics. In the ethics seminar he describes the figure of Antigone herself as anamorphotic. The "negotiation," as it were, between Adorno and Lacan is conducted at the site of Bernhard Schlink's novel *The Reader*, itself concerned with issues raised by the Holocaust. What is unspeakable in history is here refigured as what is unspeakable in an individual's history, that of the former camp guard, Hanna. Thurston, using the figure of anamorphosis, points to the unspeakable in the novel (linking it to both Adorno and Lacan). But if Hanna and Antigone are both anamorphotic figures, nonetheless they must be distinguished. Hanna holds to her truth steadfastly, but this is not under conditions that leave her a free choice in the matter. There is for her a certain impossibility of representation but that is far from any metaphysical grandeur. Thurston reads her case "as a desperate, self-annihilating struggle to consolidate the domain of the ego." They both figure as transgressors of *jouissance*, but how differently! Which leaves us with a set of questions about the nature of sublimation.

Graham Hammill uses Freud and Lacan to establish the political and social axis of sublimation by arguing that the poses of the painter Caravaggio's models are "formally, aesthetically, and historically queer." He elaborates on sublimation as that which might allow both a challenge to existing certainties and orderings of *jouissance and* the possibility of new orderings of *jouissance*. He argues that Caravaggio's pictures simultaneously open up the gap in the standard view (fantasy) of that time *and* use that opening to construct a different social fantasy. It is all the more surprising, then, that what Hammill identifies is the construction of a "queer space" in the work of Caravaggio. Hammill's examination of both theory and art enables him to elaborate the theory of the social side of sublimation *and* make a distinctly original reading of the artwork. The idea of sublimation proves itself productive. It is not a question of applying a concept but of enabling a thinking, this time about a practice of painting in its relation to the questioning and replacement of a social fantasy. The essay simultaneously addresses politics, painting, and theory.

Juli Carson does not make explicit reference to texts on sublimation. She reads Barthes less as a theorist and more as an artist who writes *Camera Lucida*. The artist's sublimation lies in the working out of his problem in relation to the death of his mother and the difficulty of finding her again in any photograph. It is a bold reading of Barthes whose writing is read as performance and whose work as an artist allows a shift of position.

This volume explores not only the theory of sublimation but also the *sinthome*. The latter is Lacan's new theory of artistic creation, developed in the mid-seventies. Now he relates art to the symptom, using the old French version of the word—*le sinthome*—in this context. If sublimation took us beyond the pleasure principle, the *sinthome* takes us way, way beyond it. Whether it concerns neurosis or psychosis, *jouissance* now has a crucial role in how human beings are psychically organized. The last four essays of the book take up the new status of *jouissance*, something that has not yet been introduced to the English-speaking world in a wider art context.

Two Lacanian analysts use their clinical and their research experience both to clarify and develop the theory. Franz Kaltenbeck explains both theories, of sublimation and the *sinthome*, and clarifies their differences in relation to the Real in unexpected ways. Geneviève Morel carefully presents the argument of Lacan's seminar on Joyce, filling in the gaps and developing the theory of the new kind of nonimaginary ego that the *sinthome* is.

My own contribution shows how this theory affords an understanding, not just of a written text, but of certain visual texts. Lacan has argued that a nonoedipal structure can be put in place without paying the price of psychosis. My claim is that this understanding provides a new way of analyzing certain contemporary works of art and film. The essay on Joel-Peter Witkin demonstrates, through a reading of the pictorial text, that Witkin's pictures serve the same function for him as writing does for Joyce. The essay on Cronenberg's *Crash* shows how the film itself functions as *sinthome*. This may seem to be an illegitimate move to some readers. How can the analysis of Joyce (albeit not in person) be used for the analysis of a filmic text? The justification does not depend on the content of the film alone—after all, how many analysts have "analyzed" Hamlet? Rather it concerns the way in which the film is constructed at all levels and the effect that this has on the spectator of the film. This is to reassert the belief in the common psychical space that written and filmic texts share with both psychoanalytic theory and the spectator.

The obvious differences between Joyce's writings and the film *Crash* give rise to a further set of questions. Where there is a real divergence, must Lacan's theory always take precedence? There are times when we should remind ourselves that Freud told us to turn to the poets when psychoanalytic understanding fails. *Crash* puts pressure on the very theory that recognizes it as a nonneurotic *and* nonpsychotic solution to the problem of psychical organization. To go beyond the argument of the present essay, some of what is going on in *Crash* has no parallel in Lacan's Joyce. In *Crash* there is a group effect of the *sinthome*, and the *sinthome* is worked out at the level of sex. This takes us forward in two important ways. First, there is the question of the conditions under which the ensemble of practices centering on crashes comes into being. Second, the reciprocity between males and females—the man is just as much the *sinthome* of the woman as the woman is the *sinthome* of the man—shows up the limitations of Lacan's conceptualization of the sexual relation within the *sinthome*. In *Crash* there is a *reciprocal* sexual relation. If you want to know about what is new in the human psyche, go ask psychoanalysis with art, together.

The Opposition to Sublimation

The Insistence of the Image: Hitchcock's Vertigo

MARK COUSINS

So successfully does the structure of Hitchcock's *Vertigo* flout Hollywood conventions about narrative and film itself that this fact frequently escapes comment. The film falls into two distinct parts and it would be possible to imagine that the first part, culminating with the death of Madeleine and the collapse of Scottie into mute depression, could be shown by itself. Imagine it: we would have a compressed but complete melodrama that opens with the discovery of Scottie's vertigo and closes with his inability to rescue Madeleine because of that symptom. Her mounting insanity, which drives her up the tower of the Mission, places her beyond the love of Scottie and the solicitude of her husband, Gavin Elster. This would be the outline of the narrative if the film ended here, and its narrative would have a completely consistent point of view—the whole film would be represented from the subjective point of view of Scottie alone. Now if this were the case, the interpretation of central issues would be able to be made with a certain predictable consistency. It is worth putting all this to the test; in the first part of the essay, I will restrict myself to the first part of the film *as if* the second half did not exist. In the second part,

I will deal with the second half of the film and its radical reworking of how we understand the first half of the film. This device suggests itself as a way of demonstrating how much work the second half of the film accomplishes against our appropriation of the first half.

This is obviously not restricted to the question of surprises at a narrative level. Of course, it is only in the second half that we learn the "truth" of the first half. But that does not contradict the thesis that the first half of the film can (and indeed does, within the spectator's first experience of the film) stand as an independent and complete film. There is no structural need to resolve the narrative further; by the moment of Scottie's retreat into wordless melancholia, a certain film is finished. This film, the film that finishes before being opened up again, revolves around a number of manifest issues. There is the question of Scottie's vertigo and its relation to both Madeleine and Midge. There is the question of Madeleine's suffering and its relation to Carlotta Valdes. Lastly, there are the questions of how these two threads draw Scottie and Madeleine together, and why they finally hold him back and push her forward toward the suicide that his symptom cannot allow him to prevent.

In discussing these questions I will respect the condition of bringing nothing to it that is drawn from the second half of the film, the film that continues after its end. The interpretations I will make are perfectly conventional and even obvious forms of psychoanalytic understanding. They could be characterized, like so much film theory, as oedipal in nature. I will make them not because I think that they are ultimately right (or indeed wrong) but to show how such a compressed melodrama will provoke such interpretations. They not only will have to be revised, in the light that the second half throws upon the first, but they are inherently limited in their purchase upon the material. The second half of the film itself suggests reasons why such psychoanalytic interpretation is limited, both in theoretical terms and also perhaps within clinical practice. This issue turns around the interpretation of the image. Simply put, psychoanalysis classes images either as objects of desire or as a field of identification. This restricts the approach to the image, but one that is exceeded by the second half of the film. However, there is no need to broach these questions yet. The proposal made here is to treat the first half of the film as an autonomous drama that sits comfortably with a certain type of psychoanalytic criticism. This should be experimentally tested by analyzing this film without recourse to the rest of the film, and only then to examine the consequences.

I

The title of the film, *Vertigo*, is not itself the term Scottie first uses to describe his condition to Midge, his old college chum. He says that the doctors have diagnosed "acropophobia," the fear of being in an elevated position. This results in the symptom of vertigo, in the fear of heights and in dizzy spells such as those portrayed in the opening scene. But even that scene left it unclear what exactly made up the vertigo. The situation in which Scottie found himself, clinging for life from a perilously insecure gutter and unable to grasp the hand of another police officer, hardly seems like the expression of a neurotic symptom. What the subjective camera shot did show, however, were two important additions. Rather than represent the space beneath him as a general precipice, the shot suggests that the space below is enclosed. Furthermore, the space is filmed as simultaneously moving away and drawing closer. The crucial shots of the space of his phobia come later and are internal to the tower of the Mission. Here again, when vertigo attacks him it is not simply the representation of height that is shown, but a complete enclosed space represented as from above, which nonetheless appears on the screen within a horizontal rather than vertical space. The interpretation of the vertigo will have to deal with the fact that the space of vertigo is a moving, enclosed space that is both vertical and horizontal in some sense. It must also accommodate the form of Scottie's dizzy spell that occurs when he is trying to show Midge in the kitchen how he intends to cure himself. As he mounts the kitchen steps he catches sight of the street outside and far below the kitchen window, and goes into a state of dizziness. He collapses into the arms of Midge, who catches him in an exaggerated gesture of maternal concern. This has happened before.

If the whole dimension of the "acropophobia" is to be treated as a symptom, one might start by thinking of it as a compromise. There is an unconscious wish and at the same time its repression through the representation of the punishment that would accompany the fulfillment of a wish. Within a "phobia," relations of desire, repression, and guilt may be variously woven into a symptom. Sometimes the object of the phobia may be closely related to the object of unconscious desire but accompanied by the affect of fear and dread. In other phobias the object of fear does not represent a repressed wish. Rather, the object of fear is a possible instrument of punishment and therefore it is the threat that causes the wish to be feared (Fenichel 1990). Sometimes aspects of the desire and the punishment can be joined together, as in the case of Freud's Wolf-Man. His passive sexual desire for his father and the fear that these wishes would entail his castration combined in his fear of being devoured by the wolf. It expressed, in a regressed and oral formula, both the sexual wish and the fear of castration. Something of the same may be said of Scottie's vertigo. The fear of high places and of falling from them clearly announces the punishment. The sexual wish is hidden beneath this, but at the same time something of that wish is grafted onto the punishment. The excitation of falling clearly recoups the sexual excitement that has been prevented any direct expression.

This vertigo that appears in the opening shots and that paralyzes him in the tower at the moment of Madeleine's "suicide" might conform to the public expectation of what it would be to "have" vertigo. But it does not exhaust the vertigo. When he visits Midge she asks him if he has had any more dizzy spells. Such "dizzy" spells represent a conversion of the fear into a physical expression of the fantasy of falling. But even here the vertigo combines the anguished anticipation of fatal falling with the pleasure of being caught, as he is by Midge and we-know-who before. The complex of relations that underlies the vertigo is exacerbated by the dimension of guilt. Obviously the symptom is made up in part of guilt; guilt for the desire unleashes the fear of punishment. The fact that the police officer dies redoubles the guilt. Now the guilt not only may lead to Scottie's punishment, but that punishment may be visited on the innocent. The punishment for evading punishment and for causing the innocent to be punished instead must be absolute. The conviction of having caused the police officer's fall and then of causing Madeleine's suicide is given a legal validation of his guilt, delivered in the laconic words of the coroner. The initial impulse, the repressed wish, wanders through a range of entanglements, through phobia, through conversion, through unbearable guilt, and into withdrawn melancholia. Of course, each of these is only itself a displacement of the wish. If the phobia still contains iconographic traces of the original wish, these surely lie in the particularity of the space of the fear. This particular space is created by shooting the interior of the Mission tower, or rather a model of the tower so that the space seems to be both lengthening and getting closer. The effect is achieved by the camera tracking back but zooming forward. Hitchcock states, "The viewpoint must be fixed, you see, while the perspective is changed as it stretches lengthwise. I thought about the problem for fifteen years. By the time we got to *Vertigo*, we solved it by using the dolly and the zoom simultaneously" (Truffaut 1985, p. 246). But nothing else of the repressed wish will be found here. That will be found in an element that is insistent, repetitious, and without meaning.

To reach this, it is necessary to go via Madeleine and her suffering. She suffers from reminiscences, but not her own. Her husband, Gavin Elster, explains to Scottie, whom he prevails upon to watch over her, that she enters fugue states in which she "becomes" Carlotta Valdes, her great-grandmother. It is a historical fact, recalls Pop Leibel, that Carlotta Valdes was thrown over by her powerful lover who also took away their child. Distraught with grief, Carlotta gradually descended into madness. Now Madeleine, whose family has concealed the story of Carlotta from her, seems mysteriously to be taking on, for increasing periods, the identity and by implication the destiny of the unhappy, the mad, Carlotta. Scottie, having agreed to follow her, tracks her pilgrimage the following day from the flower shop Podesta Baldocchi, to the Mission Dolores, to the grave of Carlotta Valdes, and finally to the palace of the Legion of Honor in Lincoln Park. Scottie enters the gallery at whose far end sits Madeleine, absorbed by a painting. He moves closer, affecting to look at two paintings on the opposite wall. As he stands behind her, his attention and thus ours are drawn to the small bouquet of flowers on the bench, the flowers that she had bought earlier. In an uncharacteristic and almost pedagogic series of shots, the camera moves forward from these flowers to establish a homology with an identical bunch in the portrait. This pair is now matched with another pair, which establishes the identity between the coil of hair of Madeleine and that of the portrait. Of course, as the gallery attendant answers Scottie, the subject is Carlotta Valdes. Both the bouquet and the coil of hair are a reference to the presumed increasing identification of Madeleine with Carlotta. But the bouquet and the coil do not, as might be thought, play the same role. The bouquet, purchased at Podesta's, is now a mystery solved; the coil of hair is a mystery posed. Even though the coil links Madeleine and Carlotta, why is it *this* link that has come to represent the link? At this point the signifier has no meaning, though it now has significance. It will require some element external to Madeleine/Carlotta to become intelligible.

It ought to be possible by now to frame an interpretation of elements of the first film. The melodrama has involved at least two lines of significance that must ultimately be drawn into a single thread. The first line is that of Scottie's apparent symptom, vertigo. It may be thought of as exhibiting traditional aspects of a phobia, namely that condition in which the phobic object has something of the repressed object of desire about it. In the case of Scottie, the object of his fear is not heights in general but a certain space whose representation is given horizontally as much as vertically. It is, in its most realized form, in the tower of the Mission church, an enclosed space, a hole that moves in a distinct way. One is drawn into it as it moves away. In addition to the fear and paralysis it induces in Scottie, it seems also to produce a swooning and collapse. This aspect of his vertigo is caught in the scene with Midge when, struck with vertigo at the glimpse of the view down to the street from her kitchen window, he collapses onto her in the pose of a Pietà. We can provisionally suggest that fear and repression of the object of his desire return as vertigo. The identity of that object is hinted at in his relation to Midge. Despite their intimacy, Midge is characterized by her independence. She has no role in his internal drama. She may have been "waiting" for him, but he isn't going to catch up. He is fixed upon a prior object whose direct substitutes are sexualized. Midge is not such a substitute, or rather could be only if the relation to the prior object had been resolved. She might be the girl-next-door, but next door is too far for Scottie. There is a work of negation here; since Midge cannot be a substitute for that prior object, paradoxically she can represent the object's *name* since there is no need for repression. When she arrives to visit Scottie in the hospital she can say, "Don't worry, Mother is here," because she is *not*, and could not be. The unresolved Oedipus complex places an absolute barrier between them. And paradoxically this is the reason she adopts the role, as much through her irony as through his need, of mother, sister, or chum, as needs be. To turn this the other way around, the nonrelation to Midge precisely indicates the continuing, repressed, and incestuous relation to his mother. This is captured at the very moment we might consider as the end of the first film. She explains to the doctor that the object of his love is dead *and* that he is still in love with her. She walks out of the hospital and out of the film, down a corridor that mirrors the very space of Scottie's vertigo, although presented firmly on the horizontal. There is neither movement nor panic, and the space remains what it is.

We can reach the issue of the mother from a second direction—that of the coil of hair. It has already been noted that Hitchcock makes a laborious point of linking the portrait of Carlotta Valdes and the seated figure of Madeleine in the gallery. I have argued that the bouquet and the coil do not, however, have an equal significance. The sign of the bouquet is already exhausted, since it finds its signification in the narrative of Madeleine's visit to the florist. The homologous nature of the coil of hair certainly links the two but plays no role in suggesting what it refers to. The coil of hair remains a mystery. Now a possible solution can be put forward. The space of Scottie's phobia is a space that could embody a young child's incestuous wish. If the space could refer to both the internal space of the coil and the space of the phobia, then it would be a space in which incestuous wishes found a definite topography; at the same time it would have been connected, by the paternal interdiction of the mother, into a space of fear. It would follow from this that his captivation by Madeleine, and more specifically by her coil of hair, is an acting out of his incestuous desire for his mother, just as his inability to move in the Mission tower is still the consequence of his guilt or expectation of punishment for the wish. Still unable to climb because of the nonresolution of the Oedipus complex, he has been able to fall for her while not being able to save her from falling.

II

Up to now, the question of the image in the film has been treated, as in so much film theory, as an issue of identification. But perhaps *Vertigo*'s meditation upon the question of the image exceeds the grasp of the category of identification. We might suggest that *Vertigo* reveals the flaw in that concept. For identification folds into one category two quite distinct issues. On the one hand, the term *identification* refers to the order of narrative and is used, in part, to describe how characters do and do not relate to each other, and how the spectator is caught up in the narrative and distributed across it, how the spectator "identifies." At the same time, it refers to a more visual order in which the film narrative is coded in, and as, images. The term *identification* runs both these senses together, and it may be that in some films these registers do indeed fit each other. But *Vertigo* hangs, above all, on the dissociation of identifications and images, so much so that it casts a shadow over the very assumption of their usual coincidence. This dissociation works at the level of names as well as images. To say that Scottie identifies with Madeleine or the image of Madeleine is not to refer to a character but to raise the mystery of the image. The name of Madeleine takes on a life of its own, as does the image. To say she is "really" Judy is not to explain relations but rather to enter them. It is not a question of mistaken identities but rather the mistake of identities. This conflation of two different registers, of the narrative and of character on the one hand, and the image on the other, has the overall effect of repressing the economy of the image since the image is reduced to being the sign of something else, of being an image of, an image of somebody or something. And of course, psychoanalytically, the notion of a sign falls oedipally and invariably into the idea of a substitute—an image, then, of somebody before and somebody elsewhere. This use of the category of identification has the further effect of hunting out the "original" for whom the "substitute" stands in. All interpretative emphasis is put upon the "original," which is thought of as the real object of unconscious fantasy. Even if the chain that links substitute to original has intermediaries, the analysis moves mechanically to the original who has always been waiting off-camera to be named by this repetitive algorithm. That is how we may claim to uncover a chain that links Carlotta Valdes to Madeleine to Scottie's mother.

It is not my point to argue that this is simply an error, but rather to suggest that it is an abuse of interpretation. It is a restriction of interpretation that is the effect of this model of substitute and original. For on this model each substitute bears a singular relation to the original but no relation to any other substitute. The subject, over time, may make a number of such identifications, but there is no series as such. To indicate a substitution is already to say "mother," or indeed any familial term. It is the structure of the oedipal as it governs an oedipal deployment of narrative. The structure of the "originals" will include a number of references and terms such as father, mother, son, daughter, and so forth. The fundamental question, however, is how are these terms themselves to be interpreted? If it is thought that having said "mother" or "father" the search for the origin is over, one can surely observe that it never began. Once the image is treated as the substitute for an original, the answer is already given. But it is a purely tautological form of reasoning. The fact is that the term mother or father should be treated not as persons but as functions or positions. There must be an alternative account that does not reduce the reality of the series and does not repress the centrality of the image as such.

Such an account would start from a consideration of the very structure of *Vertigo* as a whole. One could see the first film as precisely inviting the reductive interpretation that the second film dispenses with. In this case, it is not so much a question of simply denouncing the first interpretation as pure error, but rather seeing how the structure of the first film solicits such an oedipal response, and then seeing the consequences of its dissolution. The interpretation of the first film (in obedience to the rule that no knowledge of the second film must enter into the interpretation) has been that Scottie's vertigo is ultimately to be located as an unresolved oedipal conflict in which the symptom is a displaced repression of his desire for his mother. The sign of the mother is represented by the coil of hair on Madeleine and on Carlotta Valdes. The coil is ultimately the space in which desire and fear mix and is then generalized into heights that never quite lose their connection to the coil. Such an interpretation follows a conventional path. The question of the series is reduced to being a singular relation to the original. The question of the image is reduced to being the sign of another object. What the second film accomplishes, and permits us to grasp, is that the series cannot be thought of in this way, and neither can the question of the image. This is first posed by the narrative and the spectator's relation to it. The meeting with Judy is the last moment when Scottie and the spectator have the same relation to the knowledge of the plot. The spectator immediately separates from him and becomes privileged to the story. Only Scottie now remains as a survivor of ignorance, until finally even he detects the story behind the narrative at the end of the second film. If we accept that the second film is both an analysis and in a certain way a repetition of the first film, then his pursuit of Judy becomes a repetition of his pursuit of Madeleine. But he is not repeating an action. What is repeated is the series, which is now Madeleine-Judy. Moreover, in recognizing the series, the whole issue of the image becomes foregrounded. It is precisely Judy's paradoxical failure to fit the image that lends the image an insistent but independent role in this. It follows that the difference between the first film by itself and the spectator's reaction to the first film as the second unfolds should entail a revision that in turn should be reflected in the interpretation. Above all, such a revision will challenge the terms of identification.

This can be thought through by posing the question of the object of Scottie's desire. If read by itself the first film gives us an answer: Madeleine, though this is qualified by his vertigo that functions as an

obstacle to her. But if viewed again in terms of the second film, the answer becomes more complex. Judy is not the object of his desire but rather a potential but by no means adequate reproduction of the image of Madeleine. When dining with Judy at Ernie's, Scottie is distracted by a figure who at some distance seems to offer a closer resemblance to Madeleine. As she comes nearer the resemblance dissolves, leaving only the similarity of the gray suit. Judy and we have to endure the knowledge of the real situation. But it also revises the reading of the first film and his relation to Madeleine. That revision of our understanding of Scottie's desire recognizes that what he pursues is not an object but an *image*. This formula could still, all too easily, be taken to mean that in terms of the narrative of the first half, he needs to mold or select those aspects of Madeleine that most resemble the image of his lost (maternal) object. But this is just the reductionism I am opposing here; even if the coil of hair is underlined both by Scottie and the camera as what links Madeleine back to his

mother, there is no reason to make that coil an active cause. We should not think that there is an originary maternal coil directing the son in the quest for a substitute. Rather we should imagine that in his initial fixation upon someone, he retrospectively projects it back upon his maternal imago as an *image*, as if it were an origin. Indeed the scene in the art gallery seems to be organized to suggest this. The question of the coil comes up between an image of Carlotta and the sedentary Madeleine.

This issue of "between" is central. Scottie's relation to the image has an invariably interstitial quality. This is one reason for the importance of mirrors in the film; they double and redouble the relations he has *between* women—between the image of Carlotta Valdes and Madeleine, between Madeleine and Judy, and between Judy and anyone who might be mistaken at a distance for Madeleine. His subjectivity appears as a movement in respect to one of a pair. We might validate this by contrasting the series with the figure of Midge. She is too robustly herself, too resolved a character, to offer Scottie anything but herself. Their relationship, affectionate though it be, remains inevitably brotherly on his side, a fact and a warning that until his oedipal symptoms are dissolved he cannot be with any woman who does not relate to his own unfinished business. Midge can use neither her sexuality nor her intelligence to make him anything other than absent-mindedly fraternal. She is finally provoked to satirize his fantasies and literally to paint herself into the picture. She produces an image, a portrait that is a copy of the Carlotta Valdes portrait, with the difference that it has Midge's own head. The portrait is indeed an impossible object and has about it the status of a hybrid being, perhaps, inevitably, a sphinx. This irruption from which Scottie withdraws only seems to underline his prevailing condition—of being captivated by an image that is a result of being confronted by two images and his choice between those images.

The difference between what Scottie does and the usual account of an identification must be clear. Normally an identification occurs with an object of which the subject already possesses an imago. This is why identification so dissolves the distinction between interiority and exteriority, between intimacy and what we might call extimacy.

Identification seems to be both a projection and an introjection. This is also why the question of the image seems so vague in the question of identification. Is the "image" the external object that is introjected? Or is the "image" the image, the template within the subject waiting to project itself upon an image that fits itself? In either case, this is not what Scottie does. He pursues an object with the driven character that has led some to characterize it as typical of a whole structure of the male pursuit of women. But his pursuit of the woman must include an account of the aim of the drive in which the assumption of sexual conquest or possession must be dropped. For he pursues the object with the aim of finding an image. The "image" here is not the visual quality of an object. It is the mark of an apparition. As he approaches her, he must divide her into what is of no consequence and what is essential to her being as an image. Either he is dividing an object into its image and its remainder, or, more typically, he finds himself between two images, one of which he chooses on the grounds that it is the image of the other image.

This enables us to prise even the first film away from the oedipal reductionism of the substitution of Madeleine for the lost maternal object. The coil should not be taken as the sign of that object. It does not need to be founded historically on the mother, for its structural foundation occurs in the very identification with images and it finds its application, not among sons, but among those who identify with images. It is not that he identifies with Madeleine because she has the same coil of hair (as his mother). It is rather that he identifies with Madeleine because of her apparent identification with the image of Carlotta Valdes, through the double series of bouquet and coil. Scottie may believe that this relation has its origin in Carlotta, just as we may continue to entertain the psychoanalytic fantasy that its origin points to his mother. But both occlude the real order of causality, for there needs to be a sharp distinction drawn between a fantasy of origins and the mechanism of origination. That mechanism lies in Scottie's identification with Madeleine's apparent act of identification with Carlotta. Strangely, this produces the effect of an oedipal identification, *as if* he and Madeleine are joined together by the remarkable but ultimately contingent link of hair. This type of identification tends to ground itself in the past, and often psychoanalytic interpretation colludes with this. But the real relation is that the "past" is a field of effects whose origin is fully within the present. The usual causal relation of past and present is here reversed. It is merely an extreme case of that event known as "meeting" someone, in which a mutual identification proposes itself to consciousness as an event that must overflow the present, considered as the domain of contingency, and seeks its bearings in the fantasy that the meeting had always already been prepared by the past. It is as if in some way it is a second meeting, as if the space of the meeting registers an echo from elsewhere, long ago. And, of course, the identification occurs in an art gallery.

This brings us closer to the question of image in *Vertigo*. It is an element that exceeds, and thus returns to undo, the usual ideas of identification. We can specify this by contrasting a traditional view of representation that insists that an image reminds us of whoever is absent. The likeness brings him or her to mind if not body, if not to presence. This distinction in which the presence and the absence of the object exhaust all possibilities is clearly not the distinction we need. We are concerned with a more savage and less availing account than that, which has the image being a *remainder* in the absence of the object. For what is crucial to the definition of Scottie's image is the role that is played by loss rather than absence, in relation to the image. This loss, I shall argue, is not about a "lost image" as if we have some internal counterpart to the "lost object." Indeed I have no idea what a "lost image" might be. But if we start with Scottie's typical act of dividing an image from an object, or an image of an image from an image, and so on, we can see that he works within the field of images that have been cut out of objects. Whatever lies on the side of objects is drained away. This is what it means to suffer and indeed to love images.

Scottie's object is an image and I call such an image an "image of loss." Such an image already contains the loss within itself, though it is not at all an image of someone who has been lost. In Scottie's case what is at stake is the continuous loss of the object, which is both the consequence of and is commemorated within his possession of the object as *image*. Every loss occurs as an object, but the nature of possession varies according to the aim of the drive. The relation of possessing an image takes the form of being "possessed." The subject must keep the image alive, even if the object dies. As Scottie remarks after fishing Madeleine out of the bay, "I'm responsible for you now, you know. The Chinese have a saying that once you have saved someone's life, you are responsible for it forever." She replies, "And you'll go on saving me? Again and again?" (shot 155 script). This account is of an image whose constitution bisects the question of loss. At a formal level we may connect this with the outline of an image, even to the point where the outline is all, as in the case of a silhouette. The reader of a silhouette figure is unable to decide whether the figure is all there or is cut out. The accentuation of the outline produces a figure that exists in a different register from the ground. The undecidability of the question of presence or absence transforms the figure into a figure of loss. The figure is both present and folds the loss of the object into its constitution. It acts upon the subject as that which must be kept present, must be rescued again and again. If it went, what it threatens is not a loss that leads to mourning, but rather the loss of a loss that constructed the subject, which would lead to collapse.

So Scottie's own collapse might call up the category of mourning in Freud's sense, but it has a difference. What exactly causes his retreat into melancholy? Not the loss of her as an object, for she had never been an object, had never been the aim of his desire. What he has lost is not her, but everything. More precisely, he has lost that image that had lent him a method of discarding objects. He has lost the image of her to which he had always related with the passion of grief. He had always tried to save, we may say conserve, that image through his identification, in which the work of keeping the image alive gave him a vicarious sense of animation. This places him in an odd relation to Freud's (1917) account of the sequence of the elements of mourning in *Mourning and Melancholia*. There, a sudden and uncontrollable identification with the dead beloved sets up a household within the subject that cannot be sustained indefinitely. Gradually the ego must emerge from the object's shadow, from its self-reproachful abeyance, and must unpick its identification stitch by stitch and allow the dead to die. Scottie's position is different. Already in some sense dead to objects, his life depends on his keeping alive an image and saving it from the death it has been long enjoying. In the second film he is compelled to resurrect the "image" by mortifying an object in a mad labor that seems frequently implausible, even though the audience know that Madeleine and Judy share one and the same body, that of Kim Novak. The desperate fashioning of Madeleine out of Judy acts itself out at the level of object, as a tragedy for her. She is erased in the name of reproducing Madeleine, who yet was no one else. She is trapped in a story that can be neither undone nor abandoned.

III

This relation of the loss of the image and the image of loss is perhaps dramatized by the dead body. Blanchot (1982) maintains that one property of the cadaver is that it is its own image: "It no longer enter-

tains any relation with this world, where it still appears, except that of an image, an obscure possibility, a shadow ever present behind the living form which now far from separating itself from this form, transforms it strictly into shadow" (p. 13).

Certainly the cadaver has this relation to the image, but it continues to be linked to a subject at least through the relation of a name. It is Yorick or Marat or Little Nell. But in *Vertigo* even this relation is out of control and places the question of the name *en abime*. If we say that Madeleine is "really" Judy, we have to think that both of them are Kim Novak. And who is *she* really? The narrative gnaws away at the membrane that separates it from the film's production. The name, like the image, escapes the narrative's capacity to control it. We have already argued against reducing the image to an original. No longer should an origin be located in the maternal body, although it is not the case that it is not the maternal body. The terms *origin* and *substitute* should be displaced by the idea of a series, which in this case is the image of Carlotta Valdes, Madeleine Elster, and Judy, once the coil of hair is in place. But it also has to include the image of Kim Novak, whose image includes all the others. What is true of these images is true of the names. Kim Novak not only plays Madeleine (as does Judy), but becomes part of the issue of reference that the film uncovers in the second film. There, the film is both a second narrative and, as it were, an analysis of the whole film. The question now is not who does the name of Madeleine refer to, but rather how the film has altered the question, one might almost say, the concept of reference.

This idea of the "image of loss" might be easier to grasp if one thinks about it in respect to time. It takes its bearings from a dire temporal space. If the image is not to be seen as a representation of a person, or indeed the sign of another person, and if it indicates a series, then we could say that the image is an emblem or a device. On one side it has a heraldic dimension, announcing the coming of whomever or whatever the device stands for; the image is "in the name of." As such it belongs to a futurity, announced, longed for, but not yet here. On the other side it is what functions as a memorial, of what alone remains "in the name of."

"About to appear" and "already departed" exhaust the possibilities of time. The image bears upon the future and the past, and *nothing else*. Above all, *there is no present*. None, not a split second, just
the split. This is the condition of the image as the image of loss, and
it gives rise to its characteristic affect—that intermingling of longing
and melancholy. The object of longing no longer arrives, any more
than the object of melancholy dies. The image is no longer a representation of an object who acts as the cause/effect of this affect. The
affect belongs to the order of the series. In the case of Scottie in the
first film, we have shown how Madeleine becomes the object of his
passion because she may be said to belong to a series, or rather that
becoming the object of his passion, she at once belongs to a series. In
this reading one could trace the series to an origin (the mother). Or,
one could treat the series itself as the originating structure. More
precisely, one could say that the image of Scottie's passion installs itself
in an interstitial moment between the terms of the series—between
Carlotta Valdes and Madeleine, between Madeleine and Judy, and
between Judy and Kim Novak, as the series extends beyond the narrative into the spectator's own repetition of the series. This process
of repetition or imposition of the series is firstly presented as a blunt
melodrama. The first film retains the illusion of an origin (mother)
and a resolution (death of Madeleine). But the second film is not
merely a continuation of the narrative of the first film; it is a reworking and transformation of that first film. The issue of the serial image
is brought forward and incarnated in the figure of Judy. She bears the
paradox, being of herself only when she fails as an image of herself,
and succeeding as an image of herself only when she is not herself.

This has a fatal consequence. She becomes the completed image
for Scottie only after a last and final struggle. Defeated by the gray
suit, the black shoes, and the blond hair, she returns to the hotel where
Scottie, waiting impatiently in the corridor, sees her at a distance, and
sees her as perfected. She begins to walk with that distinctive delib-
eration, each step falling exactly in front of the last, lending her a slow,
heavy sway. At the same time she is bathed in green electric light.
But all this is premature. She is not finished and Scottie implores her
to add the coil of hair—a means of completing Madeleine—just as

Judy had used the coil of hair in the gallery and in Scottie's flat after jumping into the bay, to establish the essential trait of Madeleine. But the coil is not the only object to return. Following the same logic in which Judy is negated as Madeleine, she now puts on the jewels that were supposed to belong to Madeleine. From the point of view of Judy, there is no real difference between the coil of hair and the jewels. Having assented to the suit, the shoes, the hair color, the coil of hair, having had to revert to her portrayal of Madeleine, she might as well complete the picture and wear Madeleine's jewels, those jewels inherited from Carlotta Valdes. But from the point of view of Scottie, there is every difference between the coil of hair and the jewels. The coil of hair designates the series of the image of loss. The jewels, however, belong to Madeleine *qua object*, rather than Madeleine *qua image*. They cannot belong to Judy *qua object* as she becomes Madeleine *qua image*. There is an asymmetry between the attributes of objects and the attributes of images. Scottie is reminded of this by remembering the portrait of Carlotta Valdes. Paradoxically, at this moment the nature of a portrait and the nature of an image are in complete variance with each other. A portrait refers to an object, it is a portrait of. . . . An image refers to another image. In completing the portrait, she has destroyed the image. In the gap between the portrait and the image, Scottie is able for the first time to think and to detect. Wearing the jewels, she is no longer what she should be; she is now a portrait of Madeleine rather than an image of Madeleine. In getting what he thought he wanted, and more, he must for the first time pose the question of how he got it. The answer must teach him how his desire has been exploited to mask an entirely different story: that of the criminal plans of Gavin Elster. She (who?) is now the perfect image, but she is an image of the wrong object. There might be several ways of thinking about this—the completion of the portrait as a destruction of this image. In Lacanian terms, one might be tempted to think of it as the moment of the intervention of the real, the anamorphotic moment that destroys the certainty of the picture. Here, paradoxically, that anamorphotic moment occurs when the portrait is finally enabled to have its *ordinary* reference. The irruption of the ordinary, by restoring the regime of the object, disrupts the image. The perfect image sitting in the hotel room who bears the name of Judy is the image of the wrong object. She must be the object who lured him into a passion for the image, rather than the image for whom he constructed a passion.

Scottie has been discussed in the literature in terms of many pathological states—scopophilia, sadism, and so forth. But in fact there is nothing to say about Scottie's pathology, even about his relation to images. If we have been treating the second film as the analysis and elucidation of the first film, it is time that we take the second film further. It both repeats and analyzes but there is one question that needs to be posed of the second half, for it does not pose it itself. If the story of Scottie's passion in the first film is the effect of Gavin Elster, the figure of Elster becomes important not so much as a character but as the synthesis of a number of structural elements. He has a small role, but this merely assists in forgetting the "implications" of Gavin Elster. He is in fact master of the script within the script of the first film. From his vantage point of introducing Madeleine to Scottie, he is the author of her words and director of her actions. It is Gavin Elster's narrative seduction, not Madeleine's, for which Scottie falls. Character, actor, scriptwriter, and director, Gavin Elster plays all these *within* the narrative, despite Scottie's ignorance. And our ignorance. For we become a party to the "true" structure of the first film only in the second. But this should prompt the question of who is Gavin Elster in the second film. A certain type of criticism would be disposed to identify Hitchcock, on the grounds that in the first film Gavin Elster was an allegory of the director, and if the second film is an analysis of the first, then Gavin Elster should be unmasked as Hitchcock. But this identification is too direct and turns the director not only into the origin of the film but of the complex of the image itself. We are concerned precisely with what it is in the image that escapes comprehension even as it captures the subject.

IV

Like many modernist works, *Vertigo* can be seen to double its narrative with another that speculates upon the nature of the medium. This

commonplace of criticism has to be refined in this case. The specula-
tion does not appear as an irruption or as a supplement that displaces
the narrative as an exclusive focus. It is rather an overlay, which, while
doing nothing to disturb the narrative, intervenes at another level. It
is as if the narration of the film inadvertently breeds such another level,
moving beyond the story while remaining within an expanded field
of reference. The story is one of those stories, or rather two of those
stories, that cannot be told without inciting a series of references
outside the purely diegetic code. If the question of who is Madeleine,
who has played Madeleine, is asked, the answer cannot simply be Judy.
The name of Kim Novak, whoever she may be, inevitably circulates in
an economy that exceeds the narrative but yet is produced by the narrative. If Gavin Elster is the director of the narrative of the first film,
who is the director of the whole of the film including Gavin Elster?
And what relation does he have to the portly figure glimpsed passing
the office of Gavin Elster? And finally, the critic/spectator who perhaps
has watched the film more than many times: What of him? The film
has generated an economy that passes beyond its own narrative in a
movement that can be regarded as a reversal of *mettre en abime*. This
itself, this mechanism, is a very precise mechanism; it does not rely upon
a premodern invocation of allegory, nor does it rest upon an avant-garde
technique of alienating the viewer from being a spectator. Indeed in
some sense it continuously intensifies the experience of being a spectator by demonstrating the mechanism of the image of loss.

The question of the image of loss drives the whole film away from
the question of neurosis to the question of the entanglements with
the image. This is certainly a condition with a definite economy, but
it is one that works against the logic of neurosis. It may be, as the
film so adroitly plots, a condition designed to appear initially as a
neurosis. After all, neurosis appears above all else as a narrative. The
psychoanalytic device of the case history has, in the twentieth century, established itself as a canonic form of narrative. The story of a
wish and the defense and repressions that act against it provides a
narrative structure that not only organizes the telling of the tale, but
provides secure points of anchorage for its interpretation. For this

reason revisionist readings of case histories have to confront, firstly, not the overall interpretation but the gaps, elisions, and footnotes of the representation itself. *Vertigo* undoes itself as it unfolds. But this fact leaves open the question of what this process might be. Starting with Scottie, instead of a study of neurosis we have a study of someone who pursues an image as if it were an object and who converts objects into the image. What is this? If, for Lacan, sublimation is a process in which the object is raised to the dignity of the Thing, what is it to raise the object to the dignity of the Image? And what is the economy of this formation? How might we describe the passion that, in attempting to keep alive an image, is equivalent to a demand to be haunted? Is this what love is when it finds itself on the other side of the pleasure principle?

As for the film, it repeats itself but outside the sphere of repetition. It opens itself to the mechanism of its own operation. Viewed from the side of knowledge, there is an overcoming of the closure of the first film. The lure, positively the drug, of that first film, with its capacity to induce amnesia as to its own conditions of engagement, is superseded by an investigation of the appearance of such a story— Gavin Elster's criminal genius in finding a recipe that will cook up an alibi in the form of Scottie, and then Scottie's tyrannical compulsion to resurrect that narrative. But the progressive mastery of the story by the narrative does nothing to dissolve the image of "loss." It will not be interpreted away. Indeed the completion of the transformation of Judy in the image of Madeleine by the crowning addition of the coil of hair bestows a circumstance of awe at such a return. We are and are not at the beginning (again). The figure of Madeleine/Judy/ Kim Novak—that image—walks into the room/onto the screen. The image is uncontaminated by comprehension. Surrounded by an aura of light, green light that draws the figure from any ground, it is a fully realized apparition. The image is neither dead nor alive, for it is an image. Beyond the pleasure principle and short of the death drive, it belongs to another register: it appears and it fades. This fatal flickering in a world of projection and introjection finds its sublime technology in film.

REFERENCES

Blanchot, M. (1982). *The Space of Literature*. Lincoln: University of Nebraska Press.

Fenichel, O. (1990). *The Psychoanalytic Theory of Neurosis*. London: Routledge, Kegan Paul.

Freud, S. (1917). Mourning and melancholia. *Standard Edition* 14:243–258.

Truffaut, F., with Scott, H. G. (1985). *Hitchcock*. New York: Simon & Schuster.

Sublimation and Art

2

Meaning on Trial: Sublimation and The Reader

LUKE THURSTON

The impossibility of portraying Fascism springs from the fact that in it, as in its contemplation, subjective freedom no longer exists. Total unfreedom can be recognized, but not represented.

Theodor Adorno (1974, p. 144)

OUTLINE

The article works toward a possible reinterpretation of Freud's notoriously problematic concept of sublimation by linking it on the one hand to the political aesthetics developed by Critical Theory, and on the other to Lacan's notion of the ethical. I begin by relating sublimation to the work of Marcuse and Adorno after 1945, outlining the postwar transformation of cultural values these thinkers strove to articulate. The possibilities for political and aesthetic critique "after Auschwitz"—in other words, for a criticism able to bear perpetual witness to the unparalleled historical atrocity of the Holocaust—are shown to correspond for Adorno to a specific vision of modernism (as exemplified by Beckett's drama, where meaning is "put on trial"). In Part II, I relate this Adornian perspective to a contemporary, and distinctively postmodern, treatment of the traumatic cultural aftershocks of the Holocaust: Bernhard Schlink's 1997 novel *The Reader*. Lastly, Part III introduces Lacan's reformulation of sublimation as an aspect of psychoanalytic ethics, arguing that by breaking with a certain Freudian economics (governed by the linked ideas of discharge and pleasure) Lacan allows us to address the Adornian questions posed anew by Schlink's book: questions of what is unspeakable in collective and individual history.

I

Dominick LaCapra argues for the legitimacy of putting psychoanalytic concepts to work in contexts beyond the restricted domain of individual treatment by recalling that those concepts refer primarily to "modes of interaction" and thus can be shown to "undercut the binary opposition between individual and society" (LaCapra 1998, p. 43). Few Freudian concepts can be seen to occupy this ambiguous position, this oscillation between *Innenwelt* and *Umwelt*, more oddly or uncannily than that of sublimation. Sublimation is Janus-faced, poised between the raw singularity of the drive and the polite decorum of an art gallery; it exemplifies above all Freud's urge to produce a global, all-encompassing theory, a complete account of human existence from breast-feeding to Leonardo da Vinci. But if Freud repeatedly calls upon the concept to ground the most intricate or "sublime" cultural endeavors in the dense somatic particularity of the drive—thus seeming with one stroke to subjugate all the complex historical determinants of artistic production to the random pulsations of an individual psyche—at the same time the notion of sublimation is seen to be bound up with social values, even dependent upon particular kinds of aesthetic judgment. For Laplanche and Pontalis (1973), Freud's vagueness about this social component is a sign of his overall failure to define sublimation with sufficient rigor, to the extent that it is unclear, they comment, whether the "high social esteem" accorded certain activities in a given culture should "be taken as a defining characteristic of sublimation" (p. 432).

In Freud, then, it remains difficult to tell how far the intrinsic social constituent of sublimation bears upon its conceptual status. If the criteria defining what "counts" as sublimation vary according to historical shifts in cultural values, how can the term be given any epistemological consistency? How can it be prevented from simply collapsing back into contingent effects of the values supposed to legitimize it?

If for the Critical Theorists of the Frankfurt School what Freud's work supremely lacked was any rigorous *historical* self-reflection, the theory of sublimation was surely a flagrant symptom of this lack: for with it Freud seemed to have unwittingly smuggled a whole bourgeois cultural ideology into the supposedly value-free, descriptive domain of metapsychology. The title of one of Marcuse's lectures, "The Obsolescence of the Freudian Concept of Man," made the point effectively enough: psychoanalytic theory was saturated with values entirely bound into a given historical formation, and thus its ambition to reach beyond that formation and make universalizing claims was immediately in question. However, the polemical note struck by Marcuse's title did not herald an outright dismissal of Freudian theory as outdated junk. On the contrary, it was precisely the anachronistic elements of psychoanalytic thinking that Marcuse identified as the source of its critical potential within a Marxist account of contemporary culture: in his view, Freud's work constituted a fragile, precious remnant of the Enlightenment rationality that the massive ideological hegemony of a postwar "affluent" society precisely threatened to eclipse forever.

In a comparable sense, Adorno saw the obsolescence of Freud's ideas as only one detail in a wider picture of cultural collapse and transformation in the wake of wartime atrocities, notably the Holocaust. On the specific question of sublimation, however—perhaps because it bore directly upon the aesthetic domain that was the principal concern of his own work—Adorno felt the need to be explicitly critical: the very notion, he wrote in 1951, of artists somehow transforming their libidinal impulses into socially valued achievements is no more than "a psychoanalytical illusion" (p. 213). But this brusque dismissal is immediately followed by a revealing remark: "Incidentally, legitimate works of art are today without exception socially undesired." In other words, not only is the Freudian concept of sublimation a chimera, but (even if it did have some truth in it, the afterthought seems to say) the whole matrix of social values that supported it has vanished, since what defines the legitimacy or authenticity of contemporary art is now precisely its *antagonism* to what is socially acceptable.

Thus in Adorno a straightforward polemical rejection of psychoanalytic theory comes to be both doubled and curiously unsettled by an observation about the historical shift in the social position of art. (One is reminded of Freud's famous anecdote in "The Interpretation of Dreams" about the man who gives three incompatible reasons to excuse him from having damaged a borrowed kettle: each reason might stand alone as an excuse, but together they cancel one another out [cf. Freud 1900, p. 120].)

One of the principal aims of Critical Theory in rereading Freud, of course, had been to show that what psychoanalysis had posited as "human nature" was in fact an eminently historical construct, the product of a coercive, even a specifically "repressive" civilization. And Adorno's ambivalence concerning sublimation is rooted in the different moments or emphases of this historicizing approach to Freud. If, in *Dialectic of Enlightenment* (Adorno and Horkheimer 1944), he could agree with Marcuse's (1989) diagnosis of a "repressive desublimation" at work in the postwar culture industry—whereby libidinal forces were now made to serve the interests of social oppression "directly," no longer needing to be "elevated" into some higher form or semblance of cultural autonomy—not long after, by 1951 (as we have noted), Adorno has become far more skeptical about the very conceptual basis of Freud's notion in some mysterious alchemy between the instinctual and the cultural.

In truth, the notion of desublimation, beyond merely providing an account of a perceived coarsening of postwar culture into "entertainment," pointed to a more radical historical upheaval: the collapse of a certain "enlightenment" model of the social position of art, along with a whole set of prewar European cultural values. Thus Adorno's afterthought in *Minima Moralia* about sublimation is perhaps closer to the central point of his critique than his opening salvo, with its blunt dismissal of Freud's concept as mere "illusion." Due to an irreversible epochal shift in the very status of *Kultur*, the whole apparatus of *Erinnerung*, of autonomous inward rationality, that sublimation relied on is now perceived to be simply redundant. In Adorno's view, the Freudian concept is fatally bound up with an aesthetic ideology whose bankruptcy was then being thoroughly exposed by an art he saw as "legitimate," a subversive modernism utterly unconcerned with any bourgeois propriety or "social valorization."

But the historical collapse at stake here, and due to which a model of art as the production of "higher," consensual values must be abandoned, is no mere matter of a contingent shift in aesthetic criteria. As Adorno (1966) makes strikingly clear in his famous declaration from *Negative Dialectics* that "all post-Auschwitz culture is garbage" (p. 367), in his view the effects of the German Holocaust upon European (and indeed world) culture could never be relativized or simply "understood" in some historical context. For what is permanently affected by the unprecedented horror of Auschwitz, Adorno insists, is not any specific set of sociocultural values but *the very possibility of "values"*: the formal or even transcendental conditions of sense-making, without which history itself threatens to implode, cease to be legible.

The consequent shift of theoretical focus from the semantic to the formal level is crucial to Adorno's reading of Beckett, a drama where meaning itself, he declares, is remorselessly "put on trial." In "Trying to Understand *Endgame*" (1961), Adorno grapples with what is *unspoken* in the play:

> The violence of the unspeakable is mirrored in the fear of mentioning it. Beckett keeps it nebulous. About what is incommensurable with experience as such one can only speak in euphemisms, the way one speaks in Germany of the murder of the Jews. It has become a total *a priori*, so that bombed-out consciousness no longer has a place from which to reflect on it. [pp. 245–246]

Thus the Holocaust, something Adorno holds to be "incommensurable with experience as such," cannot be rendered meaningful in any way, let alone being "dealt with" in some expository or didactic manner by an artwork. Thus the only artistic practice remotely "relevant" to its radical negativity or *Shoah* would be an appropriately bombed-out one, an art that like Beckett's drama both confronts and renders its own crisis of meaning, and thus obliquely, as it were unintentionally, "refers" to the post-Auschwitz implosion of historical meaning in the world.

This shift from the political analysis of content to that of form allows us to grasp the oft-cited *Bilderverbodt* or "image-taboo" proposed by Adorno regarding the Holocaust. This is not, as it is sometimes taken to be, a straightforward ban imposed "from above" on any mention of the Jewish genocide by the Germans, but rather an attempt to register the absolute impossibility of an adequate representation of the Holocaust, to indicate—one might say, paradoxically—its sheer transcendence of the domain of human meaning.

Any attempt by an artist to make the Holocaust into a mere scenario or theme of a work would thus be irredeemably fraudulent, guilty either of purblind naivety or—in a more sinister vein—of attempting to reduce Auschwitz to the level of just another contingent event with no world-historical significance. In Adorno's view, however, Beckett, by placing his actors in trashcans, at once dramatizes the "garbage" of post-Auschwitz culture and vividly portrays the human struggle to continue making sense in the remnants of "culture" (*Kultur*, with all its old connotations of noble European civilization, being of course heavily ironized here).

It is here, then, in Adorno's admiration for Beckett, that we can discern something of why—for all his disparagement of Freud's bourgeois "prejudices" about art—he is unwilling to discard completely the notion of sublimation (resulting in the ambivalence we glimpsed earlier). For as we see in *Endgame* and *Happy Days*—not to mention Beckett's later work, with its progressive dismemberment of the body—the disintegration of meaning on the Beckettian stage is always bound up with the body's mute opacity (with what in *Negative Dialectics* (1966) Adorno will call "the somatic, unmeaningful stratum of life" [p. 365]), its awkward intrusions onto the terrain of *Geist*, the "higher" sphere of the conceptual and semantic. Thus Adorno strongly approves of the way psychoanalysis exposes the imbrication of the somatic or pulsional in processes of artistic production—but only if it can be purged of Freud's simultaneous invocation of "higher aims," social esteem, and so on. The very metaphor of sublimation, of course, with its "spiritualizing" implications (in chemistry, the term designates the vaporization of a solid, its direct passage to a gas), perhaps carries with it a certain ideological baggage; thus Adorno's rather strained attempts to substitute other terms for it (in *Minima Moralia*, he has to fall back rather lamely on "expression").

Adorno's *Bilderverbodt* challenged artists to reinvent themselves after Auschwitz, to attempt a creative response to the radical disruption of history and human experience posed by the *Shoah*. And in his view, very few artists had lived up to this challenge; perhaps Beckett and Schoenberg had done so, obliquely and cryptically, by forging new languages in drama and music that paradoxically sought to "inhabit" the bleak placelessness left behind. As has often been pointed out, however (particularly by Marxist critics), these art forms were in fact drastically restricted to elite audiences, far removed from a popular aesthetic terrain almost entirely dominated by the stultifying products of the "culture industry." One of the greatest challenges facing an artist who might wish to address wider cultural questions relating to the memory of the Holocaust in Germany today—Bernhard Schlink's *The Reader* was published in 1997, half a century after the end of the war—would thus be to engage with this wider audience, without at the same time sacrificing the force of Adorno's stark refusal to comprehend or contemplate any "meaning" of Auschwitz.

II

Before we turn to Schlink's work, we should first clarify some of the links between psychoanalysis and Critical Theory we will use in our reading. Why, in the first place, should the concept of sublimation be related to the questions of trauma, memory, and mourning usually invoked by theoretical work on the Holocaust? In Freud, processes of working-through trauma or loss through the redistribution of libidinal investments (such as mourning) are sharply differentiated from the "drive destinations," where endogenous libido is channeled into symptoms, say, or via sublimation into cultural activity. However, a closer look reveals that both these moments in Freudian theory are governed by an identical problematic: that of *discharge*, of the safeguarding of "topographical" integrity against disruptive libidinal or mnemic excess.

It was this latter aspect of Freud's notion of sublimation, of course, that Adorno most objected to, seeing the idea that art could be a "pacification" of desire as the flimsiest of bourgeois prejudices. Just as art could never redeem or "mourn" the unimaginable horrors of Auschwitz, equally for Adorno could it in no sense abolish or reduce the intractable density of the human body by somehow elevating it to a notional realm of pure, transparent spirituality. Indeed, the agonized, suffering body of the victim tortured in the Nazi death camps emerges in *Negative Dialectics* as the ultimate form of resistance to idealism, a pure figure for the materialist refusal of ideological coercion.

In an article entitled "The Politics of Memory in Contemporary Germany," (1996) Michael Geyer describes the importance given to the same economy of discharge in postwar German opinion:

> Progressive Germans of the educated class believed firmly in the possibility of improving the nation, for which a working through of the Holocaust became the cornerstone. Their conviction was, and to a point still is, that a full and truthful account of the evils of the German past would lead to a more conscientious and more enlightened present and serve to guide future-oriented action. [p. 176]

A quasi-Freudian *Durcharbeitung* ("working-through") is made the condition of a general break with the past and of cultural reinvention, in a vocabulary permeated with the classical terms of *Erinnerung* (truth, conscience, enlightenment). Geyer (1996) tells how in fact this high bourgeois model of inward self-reflection resoundingly failed to have any impact on public memory, in contrast to the dramatic effects produced by a television docudrama entitled *The Holocaust*, broadcast in 1979. For all the cultural authority given to Adorno's *Bilderverbodt*, in the event it was mass-media images that "recaptured and brought into the open a memory that had been excised from public life" (p. 176).

Returning to Marcuse's terminology, we could identify this an-amnesis as the product of a desublimated culture—which in this instance, however, would appear to have been anything but "repressive." It is a televised narrative, with all its spectacular and easy legibility, that triggers off the recollection of repressed—or at least unacknowledged, negated, unspoken—memories in the German populace, not the lofty injunction to immerse oneself in thorough historical research in order to ascertain the truth through autonomous rationality. As Geyer emphasizes, what was important in this social "return of the repressed" was the restoration of a certain narrative *intelligibility*, as the audience watched the events of the war move toward the inevitable conclusion of Nazism, the Holocaust: the trauma of following the story was also for many a disturbing but ultimately liberating form of self-recognition.

"At first I wanted to write our story in order to be free of it," muses the narrator at the end of Schlink's *The Reader*, as he reflects on his own relation to the tale, to "our story" (which in a deliberate ambiguity may involve an "us" beyond the couple in the love story, beyond even a collective cultural identity in modern Germany). Although this desire for self-liberation through writing fails to produce any inspired, Proustian flow of memories and it is only later—when, as he puts it, he has "made peace" with "our story"—that the narrator is able to complete his account, he is nevertheless still inclined to situate the same impulse as the force motivating his writing: "Maybe I did write our story to be free of it, even if I never can be" (Schlink 1997, pp. 215–216). As we have seen, to seek to break free from the memory of the Holocaust by giving it a new, truthful intelligibility through art is, for Adorno, as vain and delusional as to attempt to sublimate or ennoble the brute somatic drive by writing an opera. If Schlink's narrator feels that he can never free himself from the traumatic story told in *The Reader*, the novel itself remains above all the tale of a quest—on both an individual and a national scale—for a certain liberation from guilt-ridden and paralyzing memory. As a seasoned writer of crime novels, Schlink is well equipped to make the tale—of a love affair between the narrator and an older woman, who then reappears as a defendant accused of Nazi war crimes—into an intensely gripping one ("As compelling as any thriller," writes a reviewer in *The Times*). As its title might already suggest, the novel's "readerly" quality (to invoke Roland Barthes' [1970] term) is to be a crucial element of how it thematizes the unspeakable or incomprehensible: Auschwitz.

The story unfolds in an alternating rhythm, between the desire to read and the desire to avoid reading, between a passionate impulse to discover and the turning-away in horrified or guilty revulsion. At the outset, the narrator enrolls with other law students in a seminar on the Nazi death camps "out of sheer curiosity," driven by a compulsive urge to comprehend and thus, he thinks, to do away with, annihilate, the dark secrets of history: "Exploration! Exploring the past! We students in the camps seminar considered ourselves radical explorers. We tore open the windows and let in the air, the wind that finally whirled away the dust that society had permitted to settle over the horrors of the past" (p. 89).

Even in this atmosphere of naive juridical zeal, however, the narrator already begins to ask himself whether it is actually possible to comprehend the Holocaust in this one-sided, "hygienic" manner, or whether it is not rather "something in the face of which we can only fall silent in revulsion, shame and guilt" (p. 102). Throughout *The Reader*, the figure of reading or understanding is linked to a recurrent image of the *face*: looking in the face, facing up to the truth. The effort to "call to account," to make visible or legible the true face of things, is constantly countered in the novel by the emergence of what a subject cannot face, what causes her or him to turn away or fall silent.

As we saw, for Adorno the unpresentable face of Auschwitz has consequences for representation or *Darstellung* in general, so that it can be addressed in art only through some radical interrogation of the semantic protocols of cultural tradition, a *mise en cause* or putting on trial of meaning itself. How, then, can so readable or readerly a text as Schlink's, light years away from the austere barrenness of Beckett's stage, be held to participate in the same gesture of associating the traumatic memory of the Holocaust with a crisis in the very production of human meaning?

The Reader collapses the distance—vertiginous, perhaps, but also strangely reassuring—between a horrifying other (named "Auschwitz") and the present moment of our ordinary reading selves caught up in the pursuit of coherent meanings—a pursuit that for Adorno, of course, was driven by a rationality compromised by its "entanglement in blind domination" (Adorno and Horkheimer 1944, p. xvi). If Schlink's novel refuses to conform to the Adornian prescription for art after Auschwitz—that it should amount to a formal subversion of reading as such—this refusal is part of the book's postmodern close-up: the banal everyday struggle for semantic consistency, the book seems to propose, can tell us as much about the Holocaust as the bleakest modernist fragment. What emerges most powerfully in *The Reader* is how the guilty shadow of the *Bilderverbodt*, of the unspeakable in German history, can be given a singular new inflection, perhaps even reimagined, by being brought into contact with the unspeakable as it figures in an individual's history.

Schlink's novel oscillates between opposing poles in its account of how individuals envisage and strive for a consistent semantic world: on one side, the acceptance of responsibility (often figured by the metaphor of facing, turning one's face to, the truth); on the other, the safeguarding of the structure or topographical coherence of an identity. Hanna's character is irrationally and pathologically committed to the second of these poles, her need to conceal her illiteracy overriding all other demands, however "ethically" binding; yet in all other respects she unhesitatingly faces up to the truth of her wartime activities as camp guard. "She accepted that she would be called to account," thinks the narrator

> and simply did not wish to endure further exposure. She was not pursuing her own interests but fighting for her own truth, her own justice. Because she always had to dissimulate somewhat, and could never be completely candid, it was a pitiful truth and a pitiful justice, but it was hers, and the struggle for it was her struggle. [pp. 132–133]

Hanna's "truth" is necessarily untranslatable, singular, cannot endure exposure in the public arena of the war crimes tribunal. Her lifelong secret has rigorously determined all her significant "choices," thus effectively depriving her of the freedom to choose them, to be the free subject of her actions. When she declares to the judge that she had "no alternative" to acting as she did, she is speaking truthfully about the structure of her life, telling "her own" truth; but in court, of course, as soon as this truth emerges it twists into Kafkaesque self-indictment.

If Hanna's way of accounting or making sense is presented in *The Reader* as a singular pathology, something necessarily distant from any public scene of intelligibility, how does the novel move beyond that pathology toward an interrogation of sense-production in general? In an anguished effort to define his own position in the trial, the narrator admits that he is obliged to accuse Hanna of war crimes, but has to add, "But the finger I pointed at her turned back to me" (p. 168). Again, a Kafkaesque reversal turns a position of moral security or integrity into its opposite, an admission of guilt. The narrator feels responsible, compromised, complicit because of his emotional investment in Hanna; more significantly, he is haunted by a sense of having betrayed her, of not responding to her authentically: "I didn't know how to face her," he is forced to admit.

What is at stake in this guilty sense of inauthentic emotion? The central moral question of *The Reader* is very clearly legible when the narrator, wishing to discuss Hanna's case with his academic philosopher-father, has to book an appointment alongside the students. "You can come any time," his father assures him as they part, but the son gives little credit to this thin semblance of paternal affection: the father has never allowed his relationships with his children to produce the slightest disturbance in his well-ordered academic life. The narrator remembers their talk about the freedom of the human subject, with the father speaking only in strictly philosophical terms, as one of the rare moments of contact between them. The crucial point here is that the father's emotional inauthenticity is defined by his refusal to *open to the other*, as he complacently chooses to guarantee the familiar semantic shape of his world by closing off the unpredictable possibilities entailed by any real emotional investments.

This refusal to open onto or confront—to face up to—an otherness lying outside the secure confines of self-identity returns through-

out the book as an index of ethical failure. At two crucial points in
the narrative, this failure is exposed by a question: firstly when Hanna
suddenly asks the judge what *he* would have done in her place; the
"hapless and pathetic" answer completely fails to do "justice" to the
moral weight of the question (pp. 110–111). The second decisive
question comes at the end of the novel, when the narrator is asked
why he never wrote to Hanna in prison; he is unable to answer. He
admits to himself that he had confined Hanna to a "niche" in his life,
able to safeguard a certain structure of subjective experience by not
having to face her directly (in a letter, for instance). Like her, in one
sense, the narrator shapes his world in order to leave intact the essential coherence of identity; but his choice is more like his father's
than Hanna's: not so much a desperate attempt to sustain an identity as a lazy preference for what is familiar and causes least trouble.
By contrast, Hanna's attempt to salvage her fragile identity has the
dignity of a struggle for truth: an all-or-nothing, uncompromising
struggle. In order to conclude our consideration of *The Reader* and
sublimation, we have to turn to Lacan's reinterpretation of that concept in terms of psychoanalytic ethics.

III

"The question of ethics is to be articulated from the point of view of
the location of Man in relation to the real": Lacan's (1959–1960) remarks at the beginning of his seminar on *The Ethics of Psychoanalysis*
announce an attempt to think the ethical not by way of an examination of any normative model of morality but via a radical disruption
of representation (p. 11). Later in that seminar he seems to echo these
opening comments when he introduces the motif of anamorphosis,
which turns precisely on our "point of view," referring to Holbein's
famous painting *The Ambassadors*. The painting, Lacan claims, dramatizes a visual antagonism or nonreciprocity—which he will restate
in 1964 as "the split between the eye and the gaze" (pp. 67–68)—a
radical nonequivalence between two points of view; an "optical transposition" is required so that "a certain form that wasn't visible at first

sight transforms itself into a readable image" (Lacan 1959–1960, p. 135). The anamorphic blot is not part of the picture, in the sense that it remains indecipherable so long as we remain in position to "read" the overall image; it only emerges as an allegorical *memento mori* when we switch to a viewpoint so oblique to the main picture as to render it, in turn, opaque.

If we turn to a second artistic example used by Lacan in *The Ethics of Psychoanalysis*, we can begin to see how these ideas might bear upon our efforts to read *The Reader*. The ethical dimension at stake in psychoanalysis is perfectly encapsulated, in Lacan's view, by Sophocles' drama *Antigone*, a distillation of the very "essence of tragedy." Following in a long tradition of thinkers, Lacan picks out the sublime figure of Antigone herself, who—with her "unbearable splendor," her blinding *éclat*—exemplifies the essential dimension of psychoanalytic ethics: the absolute intransigence of the subject's desire, its intractable singularity (pp. 243–287). In this dimension we are made to witness the tragic nonequivalence of *Atè*, or destiny, and any benevolent morality. But what we also encounter there, Lacan stresses, is a radical disruption of meaning, a *mise en cause* of signification itself. The "fascinating image" of Antigone is *anamorphic*—that is, incompatible with ordinary legibility: "Seen from the outside by us . . . she appears as the victim at the center of the anamorphic cylinder of the tragedy. She is there in spite of herself as victim and holocaust" (p. 282). There is an obvious sense, if we pick up on the resonance of this last term, that Lacan's image of the text as "anamorphic cylinder" could be transposed to *The Reader*. Hanna is as fatally "self-willed" as Antigone, and, like her, appears on the scene of public interpretation as an anamorphic image, impossible to read or account for. Schlink's writing repeatedly dwells on the visual image of the lone defendant in the courtroom, mimicking cinematic point-of-view shots as it traces the narrator's gaze. At the moment when he sees Hanna's face bearing "an expression I cannot read at all" (p. 79), we are given an almost exact equivalent of Lacan's anamorphic blot. The naive epistemophilia of the law students, their urge to decipher and devour the full text of German history, is radically at odds with an illegible anamorphosis disfiguring that text: an unspeakable truth, whether that of the incomprehensible atrocity of genocide or of the taboo, never-to-be-spoken secret governing Hanna's destiny.

With this Lacanian *reprise* of sublimation via anamorphosis, we are clearly a long way from Freud's tentative sketch of a culturally mediated libidinal discharge. If Adorno's chief objection to the latter idea was, as we saw, its implicit claim that art somehow functioned to restore a repressive bourgeois order that might otherwise have buckled under the strain of instinctual revolt, we could see in Lacan's initiative a possible response. By conceiving of sublimation not as an economy of pleasure (the Freudian "pleasure principle" being structured around the restoration of equilibrium through discharge) but one of *jouissance*—of the "*jouissance* of transgression," to quote the title of one session in Seminar VII (pp. 191–204)—Lacan shifts from a model of libidinal pacification to a figure for the disruptive effect of the drive on the order of meaning, of reading.

If we turn to Schlink's novel, we find it addressing some of these questions. The war crimes tribunal is presented as fulfilling a precise social function: that of regulating "the intrusion of horror into daily life" (p. 100), allowing the controlled release of historical trauma through a strictly codified legal discourse. The story of Hanna (or as much of it as the narrator is able to account for) illustrates with stark clarity the restrictive, prejudice-bound nature of the "justice" administered by the court. The singular structure of "her truth," her consistency as subject, makes Hanna simply illegible to the universal juridical hermeneutic, placing her beyond its demand for a single, comprehensible, and public account of truth.

Hanna's fate, then, is testimony to the nontotality of the juridical hermeneutic through which Germany seeks to explore and reintegrate its traumatic past. The public atonement and redemption staged in the court cannot accommodate the paradox of "innocent guilt" embodied by this helpless victim-criminal, so that she becomes, like the anamorphic skull in *The Ambassadors*, an illegible stain, something to be overlooked, shut away. In the same way, Hanna's character—or better, her *figure*, the face which cannot be read or "faced" by the book's narrator—is radically *withdrawn from* this gripping novel, an element *at odds with* its legibility. Because we must share in the book's single narrative point-of-view, we are unable to bring about the "optical transposition" that would make Hanna's image and story legible. Such a narrative shift, of course, would be impossible: the anamorphic image becomes legible only at the expense of all the protocols of ordinary reading, so that we would have to be situated in *another world of meaning* to be able to comprehend Hanna's self-narrative. This is the essential point: it is a story that is *never told*, and cannot be told.

Schlink's achievement in *The Reader* is to have woven this nonstory or disfigural narrative into an eminently readerly tale of discovery and self-exploration, with echoes of Milan Kundera as well as the genre of the detective thriller. One effect of this generic and stylistic combination is to arouse in the reader a set of conventional expectations that *The Reader* deliberately frustrates or leaves unresolved. The narrative's *film noir* tone—its retrospective voiceover, elements of mystery and eroticism, criminal investigation, and so on—seems to promise a final *dénouement*, a liberating moment at which the story will at last be solved, rendered fully intelligible. Such a moment never arrives, of course—with Hanna's last, suicidal act sealing her story and the novel into a permanently unresolved, unredeemed state. Hanna's story can never be "worked through," fully owned, or finally faced up to: ultimately, indeed, it is *unreadable*.

It is important at this point to try to isolate the central ethical questions at stake in *The Reader*, and to situate Schlink's work in relation to the ethics delineated by Lacan in his reading of *Antigone*. To suggest, as we have, that Hanna is "like" Antigone, that she embodies an equivalent breakdown of meaning or legibility, is to risk overlooking crucial *structural* differences which, as we will see, relate in turn to a far more troubling "analogy": that of a certain problematic equivalence between the unspeakable dimension of Hanna's character and the impossibility of representing the Holocaust.

To read *The Ethics of Psychoanalysis* alongside *The Reader* would certainly give one ample opportunity, if one wished, to "apply" Lacan's ideas to Schlink's work, to declare Hanna a postmodern Antigone by juxtaposing the two accounts of transgressive femininity, the refusal to compromise, and so on. In particular, though, we should pay attention to the following passage from Lacan's (1959–1960) seminar:

> This then is how the enigma of Antigone is presented to us: she is inhuman. But we shouldn't situate her at the level of the monstrous, for what would that mean from our point of view? That's all right for the Chorus which . . . cries out, "She is ωμος." . . . It literally means something uncivilized, something raw. . . . [p. 263]

If he rejects the epithet bestowed on Antigone by the Chorus, what is it in Lacan's view that makes her "inhuman"? In a later session, he gives us a more precise indication: it is "because something beyond the limits of Atè [tragic destiny] has become Antigone's good, namely, a good that is different from everyone else's" (p. 270) that she meets her fate. In other words, Antigone makes an "ethical" choice radically at odds with the conventional "good" in Creon's *polis*—and this is what makes her ωμος incompatible with the human community. It is in this choice, a pure act of free will, that "Antigone affirms the advent of the absolute individual" (p. 278), Lacan goes on to claim, so that when the Chorus dubs her αυτογυωτος, her "self-knowledge" is doubled by a certain "law of self": an autonomous subjective freedom that refuses any compromise with worldly authority (one can perhaps begin to see why the figure of Antigone has been such a favorite *topos* in Western philosophy).

What, we might ask, prevents a "good that is different from everyone else's" from being simply defined as *evil*? Lacan's quasi-Heideggerian reading of the climax of Sophocles' tragedy provides the answer. When Antigone defies Creon's edict and buries her brother, Polynices, she attains "the radical limit that affirms the unique value of his being without reference to any content, to whatever good or evil [he] may have done . . . " (p. 279). This point "beyond good and evil" corresponds to the "purity" introduced to human life by "the very presence [sic] of language," in which creation can occur *ex nihilo*, through a kind of cathartic hyperbole of desire. If Antigone is inhuman, then, she nevertheless paradoxically affirms the essential value of a human *Dasein*, of human Being; and her free, self-authorized decision to do so reinforces our sense of her as an ultimate figure for subjective *agency*.

The question of transgression—of going beyond the limits of the human, beyond conventional good—is cast in a different light by Schlink's work, self-consciously written "after Auschwitz." It is not simply that Schlink's awareness of the Holocaust might make him view with some suspicion Lacan's tendency to celebrate what is "beyond the human" with such Bataillean gusto. What *The Reader* achieves should rather be located at the level of a certain *a priori*: it frames what is "incommensurable with experience as such," to recall Adorno's phrase, as a way of figuring the impossibility of comprehending Auschwitz.

What is inhuman in *The Reader* does not correspond to the emergence of a sublime epiphany or *éclat*—or if it does, Schlink's writing firmly situates what emerges in the lens of remembered adolescent fantasy, heavily tinged by the delusions and retrospective longings of the narrator. In an evocative passage, the latter remembers his lover's body:

> In the past, I had particularly loved her smell. . . . Often I would sniff at her like a curious animal, starting with her throat and shoulders, which smelled freshly washed, soaking up the fresh smell between her breasts mixed in her armpits with the other smell, then finding this heavy dark smell almost pure around her waist and stomach. . . . [p. 194]

When he finally visits Hanna in prison, the narrator's "sublime," fantasmatic memory is brusquely deflated: sitting down next to her, he smells nothing but "an old woman" (p. 195). The key phrase in the pungent recollection, of course, is "like a curious animal"—which returns us to the earlier incident in the affair when the young man disturbs his lover by playfully calling her "Horse" (thus echoing, we later discover, the nickname of a sadistic guard in Auschwitz). Mixed up with the *Nachträglichkeit*, retrospective fantasy, of the narrator's memory, there is something ωμος, "uncivilized" or "raw"—that is, inhuman. It is this dimension of Hanna's being—manifested in the aromatic real of her body and the libidinal purity of the (fantasmatic) sexual relation—that has somehow been lost, has evaporated during her time in prison, the narrator feels. The institutional soap that now makes her smell ordinary, like an old woman, marks her bathetic transition from untranslatable singularity to common humanity.

The notion that, until her painful rehabilitation in prison, Hanna is in a sense not human is crucial for our understanding of *The Reader*. Unlike Antigone, who is defined as ethical heroine by her fearless decision to take a stand against authority, Hanna is not in reality able to make a choice: it is her lifelong secret that determines her destiny. Until, that is, her only genuinely ethical act when, having finally freed herself from that secret, she actively chooses to commit suicide. Throughout the trial, Hanna's singular position is bound up with this lack of subjective agency, her fundamentally passive, stoical relation to the situation in which she finds herself. If her image is properly *anamorphic* on the scene of public justice—as well as in the fantasmatic lens of remembered adolescence—this does not point to sublimation in the sense posited by Lacan in Seminar VII. There, the concept is linked to Lacan's conception of catharsis as "purification" to become an index of absolute negativity or "nihilation," of creation *ex nihilo*: a supreme instance of desire, of the subject. With Hanna, we are dealing rather with what will become the central concern of Lacan's work in the years after Seminar VII: the singularity of *jouissance* beyond desire, irreducible to symbolic law or legible structure. Completely devoid of the *auto-gnosis*, "self-knowledge," that is ascribed to Antigone, Hanna is stranded in an uncanny, "autistic" self-identity that echoes another sense of that Greek epithet: she has her own law, defining a justice and a truth that cannot be translated, included in the public gaze.

What lies beyond the human in *The Reader* is not associated with a sublime act of will, the self-transcendence of the worldly subject in eternal Being (Lacan's para-Heideggerian reading of *Antigone* frequently risks idealizing the figure of the heroine, or even setting her up as fantasmatic object, not to say, Thing). If Hanna's fate revolves around a certain impossibility in representation, this remains strictly "ontic," an immanent condition of her worldly existence, without any ontological or metaphysical grandeur. It is here that we can begin to formulate something of the "analogy" underlying Schlink's novel. For if the inhuman dimension of the Holocaust, its incommensurability with human experience, has afforded a pernicious opportunity to lend it a certain glamour (echoing talk of the "negative sublime" by Nazi intellectuals themselves), Schlink's work lays bare such mythologization as an attempt to conceal the raw truth: the Holocaust not as a transcendent affirmation of the human will, but as a desperate, self-annihilating struggle to consolidate the domain of the ego.

REFERENCES

Adorno, T. W. (1951). *Minima Moralia*, trans. E. Jephcott. London: Verso, 1974.

——— (1961). Trying to understand *Endgame*. In *Notes to Literature II*, trans. S. Nicholsen, pp. 245–246. New York: Columbia University Press, 1991.

——— (1966). *Negative Dialectics*, trans. E. Ashton. New York: Seabury, 1973.

Adorno, T. W., and Horkheimer, M. (1944). *Dialectic of Enlightenment*, trans. J. Cumming. New York: Herder, 1972.

Barthes, R. (1970). *S/Z*, trans. R. Miller. London: Cape, 1975.

Freud, S. (1900). *The Interpretation of Dreams. Standard Edition* 4/5.

Geyer, M. (1996). The politics of memory in contemporary Germany. In *Radical Evil*, ed. J. Copjec. New York: Verso.

Lacan, J. (1959–1960). Seminar VII: *The Ethics of Psychoanalysis*, ed. J.-A. Miller, trans. D. Porter. London: Norton, 1992.

——— (1964). Seminar XI: *The Four Fundamental Concepts of Psychoanalysis*, ed. J.-A. Miller, trans. A. Sheridan. London: Tavistock, 1977.

LaCapra, D. (1998). *History and Memory after Auschwitz*. Ithaca, NY: Cornell University Press.

Laplanche, J., and Pontalis, J.-B. (1973). *The Language of Psychoanalysis*, trans. D. Nicholson-Smith. London: Hogarth.

Marcuse, H. (1989). The obsolescence of the Freudian concept of man. In *Critical Theory and Society: A Reader*, ed. S. E. Bronner, and D. M. Kellner, pp. 233–246. London: Routledge.

Schlink, B. (1997). *The Reader*, trans. C. B. Janeway. London: Phoenix House.

3

History and the Flesh: Caravaggio's Sexual Aesthetic

GRAHAM L. HAMMILL

SPECTATORSHIP AND THE QUEERING OF FORM

Can sex be resolved by a historicist reading of sexuality? Can sex be determined by historicizing sexual practices, sexual ways of being? Can historicism delimit the space of sex, the time of sex? The polemical force of these questions concerns sex and the ego. Is sex a concern for the ego—the posed or practicing ego that is the object of historical and critical inquiry, or perhaps even the ego of the historian, critic, or viewer of art? If so, what, if anything, does sex communicate? And if not, to whom, if anyone, or to what, if anything, is sex addressed?

I shall develop some responses to these questions by reading some poses in a number of Caravaggio's paintings. Caravaggio's poses are appealing precisely insofar as they oddly embody a demand that resists easy recognition and conscription by a group who wants to read these poses as transmitting its sense of group identity and group value. That is, these poses are appealing precisely insofar as they are formally, aesthetically, and historically queer.

By queer I mean, with Eve Sedgwick, that Caravaggio's poses refer to a dehiscence in the symbolic order,

> the open mesh of possibilities, gaps, overlaps, dissonances and resonances, lapses and excesses of meaning when the constituent elements of anyone's gender, of anyone's sexuality aren't made (or *can't be made*) to signify monolithically. [Sedgwick 1993, pp. 8–9, author's emphasis]

Only, whereas Sedgwick locates the material particularities of queer in the performing and performative ego, I shall argue that what makes Caravaggio's paintings queer is their relation to hermeneutics and to history—to the hermeneutics of historiation.

In essence, Caravaggio turns typology against itself. As many scholars have demonstrated, typology is a Christian hermeneutic, introduced by Paul and subsequently developed by Augustine and later Reformers such as Luther and Calvin, that attempts to read Christianity's Hebrew past as the prefigurement of Christianity's decisive historical moments—the incarnation, passion, and resurrection of Christ. In so doing, these hermeneuts attempt to form a Christian spiritual community that transcends a Hebrew sense of sociality based on genealogy. One main purpose of Paul's epistles, for example, is to transcend Hebrew genealogy and kinship through the allegory of Christ's body so that Judaism can become a world religion, in Weber's sense of the phrase. The universality of Paul's world religion is limited, however, because it establishes itself in dialectical tension with Jewish particularity and carnality. While the Israelites of the Hebrew Bible can stand as prototypes for Christianity, the contemporary presence of the Jews signals something unassimilable to the historical truth of Christianity. As Julian Lupton (1996) puts it, following the work of Daniel and Jonathan Boyarin (1993; see also Boyarin 1992, 1994):

> On the one hand, the Old Testament represents the heroic yet naive ground of modern faith that provides Christianity with its historic prototypes and patriarchs; on the other hand, the modern Jews who resist incorporation into the new covenant instantiate the unrigh-

teous [and, I would add, carnal] remnant of the historical process
who threaten to give lie to its story of progress. [p. 107]

In the sixteenth century, this hermeneutics undergoes a crucial shift.
As sociologist Norbert Elias has shown, the well-mannered, "civilized"
body becomes the allegorical referent for a civilized universalism that
offers upward mobility to the moneyed merchant classes. In supplant-
ing a political and social organization based on genealogy and kinship with an organization based on self-effacing performance, the
civilizing process repeats on a secular level the limited universalizing gesture of Pauline Christianity. And, to a certain extent, this new,
also limited universalism solves the dialectical tension between Christian spirit and Jewish flesh. In this new civility, the function that for
Paul the spirit serves is *already* rooted in the body. By grounding itself in the performing and self-effacing "constructed" body, this new
civility comes up with a relation to embodiment that always just allows identity to transcend the flesh in a kind of corporeal instantiation
of the well-known Renaissance formula for subjectivity, "I am not I."
But this new civility isn't so much a secular synthesis of the dialectical tension between Christianity and Judaism as it is a rearticulation
of that tension in two dominant modes of embodiment in the civilizing process: the civilized, aestheticized body on the one hand, and
the unruly flesh on the other.

Caravaggio's paintings take this secularizing abstraction as their
starting point. Only, rather than repeat the civilizing abstraction, these
paintings introduce a difference into the difference that is Jewish identity and that is embodied in Jewish carnality, reproducing it as a kind
of sexual *jouissance* neither contained by nor reducible to the civilizing process's organization of sexual difference. It is precisely here that
I locate the queer in Caravaggio's poses. Moreover, this queerness finds
its limit when Caravaggio submits it to a logic of self-representation.

As a starting point, let's take *The Lute Player.* If we read the score
from which the young boy plays, we can see that it is the music from
a popular madrigal by the French composer Jacques Arcadelt, whose
lyrics begin, *"Voi sapete ch'io v'amo"* ("You know that I love you").
This phrase hails "you" both as the object of love and as the one who

knows that you are the object of love. *You know that I love you.* With-out the presence of the singing boy, we could argue that if you iden-tify with this virtual "you," then what allows you to ignore the split between you and "you," what allows you to pretend with some cer-tainty that you are sincerely loved, is the lack of a split in the "I" who loves you. However, the boy's pose gives this phrase an embodied ennunciative position and, in the process, translates this knowledge into something more complex: *I know* that you know that I love you. This pose doubles the place from which knowledge is imputed to occur, "you know"/"I know that you know," and in so doing, it also exacerbates the uncertainty of the viewer who identifies with this "you." You may think that you know that I love you, so this pose asserts, but once you know that I know, the certainty of your knowl-edge is compromised.

   In effect, this pose establishes an epistemological field that splits its virtual, viewing "you" in a desire for certainty, a desire that is routed through a longing for voice. In the painting, the unused violin and the bottom score marked "Bassus" can stand as coy invitations to its spectators to join in with the music-making. But if you are lured into the invitation of the painting and find yourself in the odd position of wanting to sing the bass part along with this young boy, then what exactly are you supposed to sing? Because that score is closed, you are faced with a conundrum. To understand oneself as the addressee of this painting's solicitation is to confront an inarticulateness that is directly proportional to the coyness of the young boy's pose. If there is a coyness in the pose of the boy, it is matched by the inarticulate unknowingness of the virtual spectator, the "you" whom this painting hails.

Caravaggio's early paintings do not structure their reception through the meaningfulness of the images on the canvas, but rather through a sense of unknowingness on the part of the viewer—a sense of unknowingness that the viewer sustains through an inability to say what it is the painting seems to want you to say. Like the awkward and dumbstruck figure of Joseph, who in *Rest on the Flight into Egypt* is doubled by the head of an ass, the viewer whom the early boy-paintings solicit is sustained by an inarticulateness that these paintings produce. Within the epistemological space that they construct, these paintings present the subject's interior split as practical stupidity.

The unknowingness that this theatrical space produces is not something that one could fill out with more historical or psychological information. Instead, this unknowingness marks a heterogeneity to the space of posing which, if you take the portrayed singing as an expression of the boy's desires, turns the painting into a lure to catch you as a spectator and forces you to identify with a structural muteness, a lack of what Lacan (1955–1956) calls the "vociferated signifier" missing in both the subject and the Other (p. 305). In other words, these paintings attempt to procure an epistemological pose from their viewers, in the process procuring interpretations that will never quite overcome or assuage this loss of voice. If I identify with that virtual "you," I find myself not so much at a lack of words as at a lack of voice. *I cannot say what it is that this painting drives me to want to say, but—so the painting appears to promise—if I study the painting long enough, maybe I will be able to say it.* This experience of lack isn't a problem that the painting can solve; rather, identification with the loss of voice is the "guarantee" that this painting is meant for you.

A number of Caravaggio's religious paintings locate this voice through the topos of conversion. These paintings arrest their central figures in poses that exacerbate the distinction between being and calling that conversion narratives produce in order to allay. These paintings show posed bodies that tend *not* to follow the voice that impels group formation, and, in the process, they reconfigure that impelling voice into something potentially disruptive of group formation.

Think of *The Raising of Lazarus.* In the biblical version of the story, Jesus cries, "Lazarus, come out!" And immediate following, Lazarus walks out of his tomb, alive (*John* 11:44). But here Caravaggio's painting freezes the moment between Jesus' call and Lazarus's resurrection. Lazarus is posed between life and death, one hand falling corpselike toward a skull lying on the ground, the other raised toward a light just behind Jesus' head. The weeping mourners who look directly at Lazarus don't seem to recognize that he is coming to life, while others in the painting do appear to recognize that something odd is going on, somewhere off the space of the canvas. What counts here is not just the hailing of Lazarus, but something heterogeneous to Jesus' command.

Think of *The Calling of St. Matthew.* All three Gospels that tell this brief story present Jesus' voice as irresistible. Jesus sees Matthew and says, "Follow me." Immediately thereafter, in the next sentence, Matthew gets up and follows him (*Matthew* 9:9, *Mark* 2:14, *Luke* 5:28). In contrast, Caravaggio's painting captures the moment between the call and Matthew's understanding that he is this call's addressee. Far from being self-evident and compellingly meaningful, this voice is opaque. The painting shows Matthew pointing—to himself? To the guy sitting next to him—posed as if to say, "Huh, you mean me?"

Not only do Caravaggio's religious paintings tend to configure voice as both opaque and eccentric to what narrative would present as a self-evident command, they also present the opacity of voice as something that produces longing for an illicit, unarticulated enjoyment that we can read in the embodied pose of the one who is being called. Think, finally, of *The Conversion of St. Paul*. You will recall how Paul describes the events on the road to Damascus. A bright light shines from heaven. Paul falls to the ground and hears the voice of Christ, which no one else can hear. The voice asks, "Why are you persecuting me?" To which Paul responds, "What am I to do, Lord?" (*Acts* 22:6–10).[1] Following Paul's story, Caravaggio's painting shows Paul hearing the voice that no one else hears and arrests him precisely as he embodies his question, "What am I to do?" Surely, Caravaggio's Paul is posed *in the process of* being drawn toward the absent voice calling him to be something else. But also note: this pose of being in process is deeply erotic. The sexy repose of Paul's supine body, open-armed and open-legged, encourages us to trace out this absent voice as an embodied lover whose spatial outline the quietude of both the old man and the horse block out.[2] A visual example of Freudian negation, this quietude, along with the placement of the old man and horse, stands as a bulwark that denies the particularly illicit materialization of this voice that Paul's body appears to encourage (Freud 1925). The voice that these paintings isolate is not the one that compels an historic "progression" from the religion of the ancient Hebrews to Christiantiy. Even *The Conversion of St. Paul* doesn't simply reenact Pauline historiography in which the spiritual life of the Christian

---

1. In his reading of this painting, Walter Friedlander misquotes the biblical passage. "The men which journeyed with [Saul] stood speechless, hearing a voice, but seeing no man." This is important to note because, while Friedlander's analysis is quite accurate in its detailed explanations of how the space of this painting is organized around the "dialectically contrasted elements" of the horse's bulk and the rapid foreshortening of Paul's body, nevertheless, he does not attach this dialectic to "the powerful voice penetrating [Paul's] mind and body." See Friedlander 1955, pp. 3, 18-19, 24.

2. Especially this pose, with legs spread, appears to be particular to Caravaggio's Paul. Compare Caravaggio's Paul with Raphael's, Michelangelo's, and Zuccari's. Friedlander argues that in Caravaggio's *Conversion of St. Paul*, Paul's spread-legged, supine pose cites Tintoretto's *St. Mark Rescuing a Slave* and Signorelli's *Signs of Destruction*. See Friedlander 1955, pp. 3-7, 18-20. In the Tintoretto, the slave is supine and expressly closed-legged, whereas in the Signorelli, the supine figure—posed much like Caravaggio's Paul—has a man standing on his groin.

transcends the carnality of the Jews. Rather, these paintings present us with a voice that is opaque and heterogeneous to the diegetic space of the canvas—a voice, then, that isn't so much presented as historical demand as it is materialized *in its absence* in the male body posed demanding a particularized, absolute, and corporeal satisfaction of being. These bodies, caught up within the symbolic networks of Caravaggio's paintings, demand a certain vocalization that is eccentric to the call of historical and of narrative progression, a vocalization that has no discernible content. In Lacanian parlance, these bodies present us with a demand for voice as *objet a*.

In Lacanian theory, the *objet a* is not the desired object: exactly the reverse. The *objet a* is desire's cause, and, if anything, desire's objective is to obscure that cause. The *objet a* is the object of the drive. What does this distinction mean? While desire sustains itself by repeatedly searching for some illusory, impossible object that, were it to exist, would offer a satisfactory end to desire, the drive aims to satisfy itself by continually returning to its circuit. Hence, while desire can never achieve satisfaction, the drive achieves satisfaction through the repetition of its own aim.[3] And, in the process, the drive traces out some object—some *objet a*—that agitates desire and serves as desire's inexplicable cause. While the drive has a distinctly historical dimension, in that it traces out what a history that takes for its end some utopian communalism wants not to know, nevertheless, the drive is also tied to the flesh. Desire attempts to avoid the object of the drive by rendering it meaningless, dissatisfying, disgusting. But the drive, clinging to its enjoyment, renders this object an intrusive and fleshy surplus in the space of desire.

For psychoanalysis, voice as *objet a* stands in relation to group formation. For the good of the group, we sacrifice particularity to some general history and to the practices that support it. But in the enunciation of history, something veers away: a voice that exceeds or even contradicts its idealized meaning. It is the heterogeneity, the eccentricity of this voice, and not some sense of meaning or knowledge that

---

3. See Lacan 1963–1964, p. 179; see also Zizek 1991, p. 5.

it carries with it, that demonstrates its incompatibility with group formation. Rather than being filled with meaning, voice as *objet a* is filled out with an enjoyment that indexes a "particular absolute" of *jouissance*, as Joan Copjec (1994) puts it (p. 188).[4] It is the *plus-de-jouir*, the surplus enjoyment, both in excess of the knowledge afforded by desire and against which desire defends (Lacan 1975, p. 21).

This voice as *objet a* can't allay the sense of unknowingness on the part of the spectator produced by the aesthetic, theatricalized space of reception that Caravaggio's paintings produce. Its effect is exactly the opposite. Voice as *objet a* guarantees a gap between the future and any attempt to make it mean before its time. By sustaining this gap in the face of all attempts to close it, Caravaggio's aesthetic remains formally and historically queer.

SUBLIMATION AND SOCIAL FANTASY

The drive need not be obscured by desire. It can also change its aim from one that it primarily sexual to one that is primarily social. As is well known, Freud calls this change in aim sublimation, and he tends to make two seemingly contradictory statements about it. On the one hand, Freud asserts that when the drive changes its aim from the sexual to the social, it still retains its primarily erotic purpose of establishing a "tendency to unity" (Freud 1923, p. 45). In either case then, sexual or social, the drive attempts to master stimuli by forming the flesh into a coherent body and by projecting onto the external world whatever parts of that flesh the ego "feels as hostile" (Freud 1915, p. 136). On the other hand, Freud asserts that when the drive is sublimated, its "erotic component no longer has the power to bind" (p. 54), so that sublimation also carries with it a certain "inclination to aggression and destruction" (p. 54) located in the created object. Sublimation forms a community that doesn't *just* project what it re-

---

4. For analysis of voice as *objet a*, see Zizek 1992, pp. 116-120; Dolar 1996, pp. 7-31; Adams 1996, pp. 67-69; Copjec 1994, pp. 183-190.

gards as hostile onto some external source. This hostility also returns to affect members of that community in one way or another.

The example that Freud gives to support this antinomy is the idealized law—"the dictatorial 'Thou shalt.'" While this law attempts to establish unity and group identification through what Freud calls "desexualized libido," nevertheless this same law displays a "general character of harshness and cruelty" that threatens group unity by reintroducing a libido that is now sadistic (Freud 1923, pp. 54–55). Sublimation can lead to an introjection of the superego—an internalization of the law in order to avoid becoming the object of the harshness and cruelty, the sadistic *jouissance* that motivates the law. In this case, sublimation reenforces a collective desire not to know the libidinal occupations from which that desire is built. But for psychoanalysis, cultural artifacts need not only reinscribe the subjectifying mechanisms of social demands, of political norms. Sublimation also affords the possibility of formulating a different communal arrangement, "a different criterion of another, or even the same, morality," as Lacan (1959–1960) puts it (p. 109). To this extent, Lacan argues, sublimation is very close to the clinical structure of perversion.

It is through this antinomy that Guy Hocquenghem (1993) defines what he calls "homosexual desire." On the one hand, homosexual desire relies on "an ascent toward sublimation, the superego and social anxiety" that converts *jouissance* into a homosocial, between-men symbolic order. The particular sexual aim of *jouissance* is translated into a social aim on the condition that *jouissance* be desexualized. On the other hand, homosexual desire emerges as such in a desublimating "descent toward the abyss of non-personalized and uncodified desire" (p. 95), in a sexualization of social instincts that have previously been desexualized. In Hocquenghem's definition, homosexual desire isn't prior to sublimation; it's an effect of this very process. And, insofar as homosexual desire is linked to the inclination toward aggression and destruction that Freud argues is part of the created object, the sexuality of homosexual desire stands as a threat to the very sociality out of which it emerges. This sexuality is, as Hocquenghem rather brazenly puts it, "the killer of civilized egos" (p. 150)—including, I should add, civilized homosexual egos. At stake in this assertion is the relation of homosexual desire to social fantasy and to *jouissance*, a relation that Hocquenghem reads through the philosophical loci of the phallus and the anus. A society that invests *jouissance* in unity around one significant organ (the phallus) must also divest the *jouissance* articulated through other organs of their possible significances and various modalities. Hence, while the anus is one of the first sites for educating some soon-to-be civilized ego about bodily control through submission to the demand of the Other ("Make a poopy for Mommy and Daddy!") and about social discomfort over the gift that exceeds social expectation ("Here's a poopy you didn't even ask for!"), that education is completed when the anus is no longer the locus of social relations, when "your excrement is yours and yours alone" (p. 97). The anus becomes the philosophical locus for thinking a *jouissance* that no longer serves a social function.

The reason that this anus isn't simply philosophical is that the *jouissance* for which it comes to stand translates into a social fantasy about homosexual desire in which this *jouissance* is conflated with a "homosexual practice" that restores to the anus a social and sexual function: coming together through anal sex. Whether or not gay men are having anal sex is beside the point. As Hocquenghem (1993) writes, "Homosexuality is always connected with the anus, even though—as Kinsey's precious statistics demonstrate—anal intercourse is still the exception even among homosexuals" (p. 103). The social fantasy of homosexual desire translates the philosophical anus into a site of obscene dread insofar as it expresses an aspect of desire—a relation of desire to useless *jouissance*—that "is not merely the accomplishment of the sexual act with a person of the same sex" (p. 50). Leo Bersani (1995) names this obscene dread, this useless *jouissance* "homo-ness," and, in his trenchant critique of queer theory's trust in ego-identity, he argues that homo-ness is the somewhat paradoxical foundation for homosexual identity. Historically preceding the invention of "the homosexual," this homo-ness is a "self-shattering" *jouissance* intrinsic to homosexuality, an "anti-identitarian identity" that defines homosexual sociality through the confrontation of that identity with anti-relationality (pp. 101, 164). In other words, homo-ness is a specific version of a more general kind of confrontation with the absolute particularity of a *jouissance* that serves no social use, that threatens all social bonds. Moreover, this *jouissance* can't be read simply by reference to social practices or by reference to the egos that emerge from these practices. As we shall see, it can be read only in the subject's relation to social fantasy. Precisely how the subject relates to social fantasy and, thereby, to this useless *jouissance* depends on that subject's relation to sublimation.

At stake in sublimation is the production of objects that bear the burden of communal reality-testing. It would be easy to test reality if there were a simple distinction between an internal world of imagination and an external world of real objects. For better or for worse, though, this simple distinction does not hold. Nor is there any simple correspondence between objects in psychic space and objects in material reality. Material objects exist differently in our psychic space than they do externally; sometimes they exist only in our psychic space, and sometimes they exist only externally. To acknowledge and to account for the complexities of these distinctions, Freud introduces both the pleasure principle and the reality principle. While the pleasure principle attempts to bind the ego with whatever offers pleasure by expelling and avoiding those things that are dissatisfying, the reality principle sustains the recognition of those things that aren't satisfying and, in so doing, allows the subject to recognize the world. For psychoanalysis, this ability to recognize a world that is not simply of one's making is *not* more or less theologically grounded in some magical, though absent, signified. Rather, this ability is grounded in an initial expulsion of what is dissatisfying, what is kept at bay by rendering it "bad, alien, and external" (Freud 1925, p. 237). Hence, Freud (1925) writes, "The first and immediate aim in the process of testing reality is not to discover an object in real perception corresponding to what is imagined"—this would simply be a narcissistic conscription of the world—"but to *re-discover* such an object, to persuade oneself that [reality] is still there" (pp. 237–238). It is precisely through an encounter with avoided dissatisfaction that one comes to recognize and sustain a distinction between psychic space and material reality.

Following Freud, Lacan calls the stuff of this initial expulsion the Thing (*das Ding*), and he characterizes it by its absence, its strangeness, and even its hostility toward the ego. This Thing is what one must avoid if one wants to follow the egoistic pathways of pleasure and desire. But also, this Thing is what one must negotiate and rediscover in the testing of reality. Here lies the importance of Lacan's definition of sublimation as that which "raises an object to the dignity of the Thing" (Lacan 1959–1960, p. 112). To say that sublimation raises an object to the dignity of the Thing and not to some social ideal is to say that in the process of sublimation some object—any object—becomes the Thing by which a group gets and sustains its sense of reality.

The social value of sublimation is that, in "giving . . . phantasies bodies," as Freud (1930) puts it, sublimation can satisfy society's demand to reproduce itself (p. 79). For instance, in *The Four Fundamental Concepts of Psychoanalysis*, Lacan proposes that the social value of an icon is that it allows for the fantasy that the god whom it represents is also looking at it. The icon is there to please God, to "arouse the desire of God." Even iconoclasm preserves this organization, since it declares that God doesn't care for certain images precisely because they give pleasure either to other humans or to other gods. The artistic production of icons and even an iconoclastic backlash allows a group to participate in a fantasy that sustains it in its relation to the desire of the Other. In order to elaborate a survey of art history organized primarily by the myth of the murder of the father in *Totem and Taboo*, Lacan continues by interrogating the social value of the paintings in the great hall of the Doges' Palace. In these paintings, the social function of establishing the viewer in relation to the desire of the Other stays the same, only here the fantasy shifts from paternal toward oligarchic organization. "What do the audiences see in these vast compositions? They see the gazes of those persons who, when the audiences are not there, deliberate in this hall" (Lacan 1963–1964, p. 113). In both cases, sublimation produces the fantasy of a particular, fundamental representation of social organization within the aesthetic space that these artifacts solicit.

In other words, the social value of sublimation is that it allows a group to sustain its sense of reality by reinstating desire and seemingly ignore this threatening Thing. However, as I keep suggesting, sublimation can serve a function that doesn't simply reinscribe group reality, a group's organization of desire, but also allows for the elaboration of a jouissance that serves no social function and about which society wants to know as little as possible. Take, for example, Caravaggio's *Victorious Cupid* and its companion piece, *The Sacrifice of Isaac*. (I say the two are companion pieces in part because in *The Sacrifice of Isaac* Caravaggio uses the same boy model used in *Victorious Cupid*.) Caravaggio's *Victorious Cupid* straddles highly iconographic objects that signify the world of knowledge and power: astronomy (the globe with the stars on it), the military (the armor), intellectual production (the book and quill), kingship (the crown and scepter), and fame (the laurel wreath). But the straightforward signification supposedly promised by this iconographic mode is immediately complicated by the drape which, in partially covering certain objects and surely hiding others, turns these iconographic objects into objects of desire. The placement of this drape asks us to imagine even more objects of this world over which Cupid rules. Moreover, what invests or cathects these objects with a sense of desire is Cupid's pose. In this painting, then, objects of power and knowledge do not shine with the lure of satisfaction *objectively*; they shine with this lure insofar as they are invested with the coyness encouraged by this young boy's pose. That is, these objects of knowledge and power are invested with desire through the youthful male body. As with this painting's presentation of iconography, with Cupid's pose what might at first seem like straightforward exhibitionism turns quickly into a coy withdrawal. While this boy projects his right side forward, he withholds his left side, draws it back into the shadows, hiding his left arm and the lower half of his left leg, a dynamic of exhibitionism and withdrawal most forcefully located in this boy's exhibited genitals and shadowy perineum.

It isn't just this pose, however, but also the status of Cupid as poser that emphasizes this dynamic. After all, this Cupid is not a celestial Cupid. Caravaggio paints him as a young boy dressed up as Cupid (note, for example, the boy's dirty toenails)—a move that led Baglione to paint a rival *Divine Cupid* "in competition with [this] *Earthly Cupid* by Caravaggio," as Orazio Gentileschi explained in the famous trial of 1603 (Hibbard 1983, p. 307). Years later, still trying

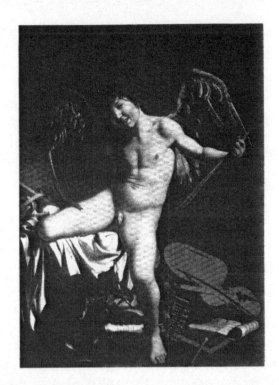

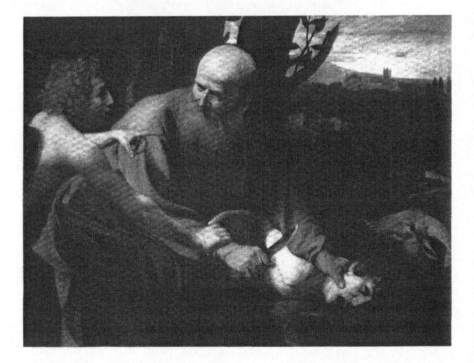

to contain and negate the "earthiness" of this Cupid, Baglione describes him as a Cupid who "subjugated the profane" (Hibbard, p. 353). Rather than subjugating the profane, though, Caravaggio's boy dressed up as Cupid stands in as a metonymy of desire—as a metonymy that is desire—for profane, worldly objects.

And not just a desire for objects: since this Cupid takes the same pose as does Michelangelo's *St. Bartholomew* in the Sistine Chapel, one could argue that Caravaggio's repetition attempts to recall a past paganism that Christianity has supplanted and thus that this painting reverses that familiar Christian topos. However, given the theatricality of Cupid's pose, I would suggest that this painting accomplishes something more radical. This young boy dressed up as Cupid creates a rift in that topos by inciting the desire for a history that Christianity has prevented, and it does so precisely through the erotic and coy body of a contemporary young boy. In other words, this young boy's pose forces an opening in a familiar Christian topos, the effect of which is to incite the desire for a history of the flesh, a history of sex, that in the early seventeenth century has yet to be written.

Whereas *Victorious Cupid* uses visual metonymy to engage our desires for knowledge, power, and history through the youthful, theatrical male body, *The Sacrifice of Isaac* uses substitution to present us with a gap. We can see this process in the two dominant movements of this painting. First of all, there is the downward motion from Abraham's arms to Isaac's head. The biblical narrative would encourage us to extend this movement so that it would culminate in the eagerly acquiescent ram in the painting's lower right-hand corner. As we know from *Genesis*, the angel prevents Abraham from sacrificing his son and has him sacrifice this ram in Isaac's stead. Certainly, the painting shows us the ram that will serve as Isaac's substitute. But between Isaac's head and the ram's neck this painting insists on a gap, a void of absolute darkness that momentarily interrupts the painting's otherwise smooth movement toward substitution. Second, there is the crosswise movement from the angel's finger to the city and lighted sky in the background (a background rarely found in Caravaggio's paintings). This movement suggests that civilization, in particular the generic representation of European civilization common to Italian Renaissance painting, is itself a substitute for the sacrifice that Abraham is about to enact. And this movement, too, is interrupted by a visual gap. The same darkness that separates Isaac's head from the ram's neck also separates the scene of sacrifice from the promised civilization that will come to replace it.[5]

While this painting presents substitutions that project forward in chronological time, more or less attempting to secure the scene of western European civilization in the background as the effect of the substitutions enacted in the foreground, nevertheless these very acts of substitution encourage us to see in the painting the presentation of an historical past through the fantasy scene that organizes the aesthetic communities that these paintings solicit. Not only do the relative positions of Abraham and Isaac analogically suggest that this act of sacrifice is itself a substitute for *coitus a tergo* between an older man and a younger boy, but also, if we reverse the movement that this painting encourages from Abraham to Isaac—more specifically from the cloaked and avoided engagement between Abraham's lower front and Isaac's lower rear to Abraham's hands, one holding down his son, the other holding a strikingly erect knife—then we can recognize in this retroactive movement a suggestion of anal sex in the voided engagement between Abraham's lower front and Isaac's lower rear. When the angel grabs Abraham's arm and blocks the knife that he is about to use to slice his son's neck, in effect this prohibition strengthens the fantasy construction that these poses suggest. It is as if the angel were offering civilization and its sacrificial economies instead of, as a replacement for, pederastic anal sex. In effect, this painting introduces a schism into a Pauline historiography that would have us understand the origin of Christianity in a conversion from Jewish carnality to

---

5. Lacan uses this painting in his *Names of the Father Seminar*, alongside commentary on the story of Abraham's sacrifice by the eleventh-century rabbi Rashi, in order to discuss the father's murderous desires for the son. For a discussion of Lacan's use of this painting, especially in his transferential relation to Freud and to the institution of psychoanalysis, see Hammill 2000.

Christian brotherhood. Through its structuring of fantasy, this painting introduces an erotic, homosexual, pederastic, and anal carnality
alongside the Jews that the angel of God attempts to terminate.

We can, I think, draw an analogy here between this angel's voice
and the lute, L-square, and compass that Caravaggio's *Victorious Cupid*
doesn't straddle: the angel's voice, like music, allows us to enter a constructed space that attempts to avoid—render unknown, even—that
other space between boys' legs. That is, both the angel pointing to
civilization and the Cupid not straddling musical instruments offer
us an opposition between the constructed and aestheticized space of
civilization on the one hand and the fantasmic scene of pederastic anal
sex on the other. What renders this opposition dynamic is the history that *The Sacrifice of Isaac* isolates and the desire for history that
the *Victorious Cupid* incites. Taken together, these two paintings introduce a conceptual difference into the carnality that is for post-Pauline
Christianity *the* fleshy embodiment of the Jew, give historical priority
to this difference, and encode it through the fantasy of anal sex. To the
extent that this Cupid coyly and erotically imposes the history to which
The Sacrifice of Isaac points, another name for this so-called *Victorious
Cupid* might be Caravaggio's Angel of History.

Please understand, though: I do not with any certainty take this
fantasy scene to be the unconscious articulation of Caravaggio's sexual
experiences. To do so would be both misleading and, finally I think,
irrelevant. I do, however, take this fantasy to be the primal scene of
Caravaggio's boy-paintings, the primal scene of the social and theatrical space of desire that these boy-paintings establish. To put it bluntly,
this scene of pederastic anal sex *is* the social fantasy that Caravaggio's
aesthetic assumes.

Remember that for psychoanalysis fantasy isn't the space of wish-
fulfillment, the scene in which we imagine our desires to be fulfilled.
On the contrary, fantasy is precisely the scene that stages our desires
as such, and that in the process represents the barriers to *jouissance*
that constitute the subject as split. To this extent, fantasy allows a
group to keep the Thing at bay. But in this act of representation, the
subject establishes a relation with the *objet a* as surplus enjoyment.

Hence, the importance for psychoanalysis of the construction of the fantasy scene: this construction allows us to specify the coordinates of our desire, the relation of our desire to its object-cause. The purpose of fantasy construction is to locate this *objet a* by reading in the habitual posturing of desire a relation to the drive toward jouissance that endless desiring unwittingly satisfies. To underscore this function, Lacan designates fantasy with the following equation: $\mathcal{S}\Diamond a$, the subject in some relation to the object-cause of desire. The psychoanalytic point of constructing fantasy is to effect its reversal, to foreground the object-cause of desire in relation to the subject's willful misapprehension of it: $a\Diamond\mathcal{S}$.

To stop analysis here, after deducing this fantasy of pederastic anal sex, would be, basically, to reinvest authority in the fantasy about which the subject of Caravaggio's early boy-paintings does not want to know. In order to effect a reversal of the fantasy scene of pederastic anal sex that we see in *The Sacrifice of Isaac*, we must understand that the acts of substitution by which this fantasy is constructed serve to render fantasy itself into a screen that can sustain the subject of the Caravaggian aesthetic in his or her desire. But in its particularity, this fantasy also demonstrates a repeated relation to surplus enjoyment that the solicited subject of Caravaggio's paintings enacts in its endless attempts to grab hold of whatever these paintings encourage it to think it wants. This fantasy may or may not tell some truth about Caravaggio, but it does stage for us in a precise and specific form a barrier to *jouissance* around which the Caravaggian aesthetic is formed: if the knife is a substitute for the penis with which Abraham is (not, as it ends up) about to puncture his son, then Isaac's open mouth stands most forcefully as a substitute for the gaping darkness that blurs the engagement between Isaac's rear and Abraham's lower front. This open mouth is not some metonym for the practice of pederastic anal sex that has been substituted out of consciousness into fantasy. Rather, sexual fantasy, as a model for aesthetic practice, stands in relation to an object that opens up onto a void. To this extent, Isaac's open mouth operates as what Tim Dean (1996), following Catherine Clément, calls a syncope, an obfuscation in an aesthetic *and* sexual field of desire which, in introducing an ego-annihilating *jouissance*, has the potential to change that ego's relation both to itself and to group-formation.[6] This open mouth serves as a kind of erotic *ex nihilo* around which history happens. In *The Sacrifice of Isaac*, this syncope doesn't continue to sustain us in an inarticulate desire for knowledge. Instead, it reveals emptiness as the emptiness for which voice as *objet a* previously stood. I should add that this presentation of emptiness doesn't make things any more comfortable. After all, when it comes down to it, anal sex isn't that scary; opening up onto a void that threatens corporeality, that divests the body of its meaningfulness, at least potentially is.

TRAVERSING HISTORY THROUGH PAINT

There's no pretense in Caravaggio's paintings that masculinity exists outside fields of desire, history, and the logics of civility. But by putting masculine posing in relation to the voice as *objet a*, Caravaggio is able to open a gap in the desire for an aestheticized and civilized masculine community. He is able to open a moment of unknowingness upon which that community's epistemological formation depends. Rather than filling out this epistemological void with something meaningful, though, rather than filling out this void with some narrative that takes the role of master-narrative, some history that turns into History, Caravaggio's later paintings substantiate the unknowingness that results from obscuring the voice as *objet a* in the libidinality of paint.[7]

This libidinal substantiality of paint makes a double mark: it marks Caravaggio's traversal of the identificatory mechanisms of

---

6. See also Clément 1994. Dean's main point in using this term is to elaborate the politico-aesthetic implications of Leo Bersani's *Homos*. Dean (1996) is interested in nuancing Bersani's concept of "homo-ness" with the notion of syncope precisely because of the ways in which syncope allows the self-shattering of sexuality to operate "prophylactically" (p. 81) in aesthetic practices—as a kind of safe-sex way to deal with the deadly dangers of *jouissance* in the age of AIDS.

7. See Michael Fried's (1997) comments on Caravaggio and temporality in his "Thoughts on Caravaggio."

Renaissance aesthetics and, in effect, presentifies the voice as *objet a* around which the space of spectatorship in his paintings is formed; in the same gesture, it also translates unknowingness—primarily a form of temporality—into a local logic of self-representation that particularizes the opening of history that Caravaggio's paintings engage. Since this voice as *objet a* serves a future contingent that exceeds the positing of any community, the force of particularization is in no way salvic. It makes no pretenses toward transcending history.

We can see these two moves in Caravaggio's *David with the Head of Goliath*. Given the parallel movements of David's left arm and his sword, one might argue that this painting presents us with a young boy whose pose brags about his having evaded the cut of castration. It is as if, by taking this pose, David were announcing that in beheading the hypermasculine Philistine giant who threatened to subject all the men of Israel, he has supplanted Goliath's hypermasculinity even while remaining a young boy. *Who cares*, so the nonchalance of the sword's placement suggests, *if the sword comes so close to my penis? I already have the phallus.* Certainly, this interpretation follows the nationalist and masculinist movement of the biblical narrative. You will remember that before slaying Goliath, David was the "well spoken, good-looking" young harpist whose music soothed Saul whenever he was plagued by evil spirits (*I Sam* 16:14–23). It is only after the slaying of Goliath that David gains Jonathan's love, becomes the object of Saul's intense envy, and sets out on the road that will eventually lead him to become Israel's popular warrior king. Having supposedly evaded castration, David poses as if on the way to becoming what the history of the Hebrew nation will have him be.

But there is more to this painting than that. There is also the dark void out of which David emerges in order to pose as an emblem of Imaginary masculine wholeness. This void isn't simply the space in which David fought Goliath, the space in which David cut off Goliath's head. Rather, this void literally avoids that historical space with the darkness of paint, signaling something more horrible even than beheading, *more unspeakable* even than castration. Compare this painting with the more generic representations of David and Goliath—for example, Pesellino's *Story of David and Goliath*, or the representation of this biblical story in Ghiberti's ninth panel for the third door of San Giovanni, or even Michelangelo's painting of David beheading Goliath in the Sistine Chapel. In each of these examples, the function of the background is to work in tandem with the pose in the foreground in order to give the story of David slaying Goliath in its historical fullness. By contrast, in Caravaggio's painting the dark void of the background creates an opening in the historical narrative. To attempt to say exactly what the background is would simply situate us once more at the position of the virtual "you" whom *The Lute Player* solicits. We would find ourselves again identifying with the inexpressible, the absent voice as desire's objective, and not its cause.

But, as it ends up, this painting does not encourage that identification. Rather, *David with the Head of Goliath* shows us what we cannot say as paint. First, by reiterating the darkness of the background in Goliath's open mouth in the foreground, this painting identifies the absent voice of the earlier boy-paintings with the void from which masculine posing emerges. And second, this painting presentifies this absent voice in the substance of paint. When David thrusts this head into the foreground, he shows an absent voice that traces out the hostile, alien, and overpowering Thing.

In a sense, *David with the Head of Goliath* accomplishes a historiographic move similar to that of *The Sacrifice of Isaac*. Both paintings portray a certain carnality in their representations of stories from the Hebrew Bible. Only, neither painting locates this carnality in the ethnicity of the Jews, as Paul does, but instead each translates that carnality into an eccentric eroticism about which the spectator can say nothing meaningful. The difference between these two paintings is that in *David with the Head of Goliath* Caravaggio also substantiates this carnality as paint. When David displays this sullen head, red paint oozes out of the structural muteness of the menacing Thing. This paint *is* the substantiation of voice metastasized on the canvas.

Doubtless, this is a standard move in Caravaggio's beheading paintings. In *Judith Beheading Holofernes* and in *Medusa* as well, the open mouth signals an absent voice, cut off by the act of decapitation, that materializes on the canvas as red, splattered paint. Only here, this red paint is precisely what engages David, what *appeals* to him even in his showy pose. Note David's red ear: it's the same red as the paint that drops from Goliath's neck. It is precisely the materiality of this voice—and not its significance—that appeals to David, that demands his attention, that catches his ear.

If Caravaggio's interest in the theatrical space of the pose is that, when the body is posed, something escapes and slips out, then in this painting we can say that this something returns, appeals, and transfixes the body of the posed boy. If this something were only a gap, then David could simply avoid it with Imaginary identifications—so many masculine poses. But in its substantiality, this something opens up a rift in the Imaginary universe of "civilized" masculinity. It substantializes the threats to Imaginary masculinity in something other than castration. It grounds these threats in paint.[8]

To put it differently, this painting shifts economies. We move from narrative, a choice of meaning and history, to the drive and *jouissance*, a choice of being. As I have argued, the poses in Caravaggio's early boy-paintings work to solicit a viewer who takes these poses as significant, a viewer who supposes these posed boys know something meaningful about desire that we ourselves can't articulate. But if choosing meaning is a strategy to keep the Thing at bay, then drive is the mechanism that brings it back, that lets the Thing rematerialize, metastasized as paint, as a consistent and agitated imposition that disturbs this choice of narrative meaning and history.

As a substance, paint stands in as the *jouissance* that serves no function, that short-circuits an aesthetic community based on *istoria*, narrative, history. To whom is this *jouissance* addressed? It may appeal to some, catch the ears of others, but fundamentally it can be addressed to no one at all. This is not to imply that Caravaggio's paintings attempt to be ahistorical. Far from it: these paintings are deeply historical, but in a way that is radically oriented toward the future.

---

8. I am here indebted to Parveen Adams' (1996) discussion of Francis Bacon's paintings in "The Violence of Paint." Adams argues that specifically painting offers a way to think about a violence of psychical deflation that is outside of the phallic vocabulary of castration so central to psychoanalysis. While Adams argues for the political and therapeutic importance of the concept of castration, her work is also dedicated to finding other models that can embody and extend this concept.

And they will remain so as long as we can watch in them the elaboration around this useless *jouissance* of an ethic that drains the body of its narrativized and grand historical significance.

At the end of a Lacanian psychoanalysis, this *jouissance* becomes, oddly enough, the site of identification. Against the notion that analysis should end either with an introjection of the analyst's supposedly healthy ego or with an acceptance of Freud's (1937) infamous "bedrock" of castration (p. 252), Lacan (1963–1964) argues that throughout analysis the analyst must embody the *objet a* in its ectopic distance from the idealized positions of knowingness that the analysand demands the analyst incarnate. "It is from this idealized identification that the analyst has to fall, . . . crossing the plane of identification" until the analysand comes to recognize the particular surplus enjoyment that her or his fantasy has repeatedly attempted to screen out (p. 273).[9] In so doing, the analyst allows the analysand to recognize this surplus enjoyment not behind but *on* the screen of the fantasy. The analyst introduces a piece of the Thing back into the symbolic order so that the analysand can traverse fantasy as an organizer of desire and begin to experience it as a way to make present the drive against which it has hitherto defended.

For Caravaggio, this crossing translates the historical opening produced by his paintings into an identificatory logic that situates the aestheticized body in relation to a violence of representation. As is well known, the head of Goliath that David shows us is Caravaggio's self-portrait. And if, as critics have noted, the letters on David's sword that read *M AC O* stand for *Michel Angelo Caravaggio Opus* (Moir 1982) then we could speculate that this sword suggests that the work of painting cuts the painter from his body, turns him into paint. What Caravaggio's self-portrait as Goliath realizes is that the painter doesn't have the voice either. The substantialized voice oozes from his neck, too. But, rather than sustaining a relation to the *ex nihilo* of history, this painting translates that *ex nihilo* into a point of identification.

---

9. For a discussion of identification with the "fall of the object," especially in relation to Lacan's crucial notion of the pass, see Dunand 1990; see also Shepherdson 1994.

Caravaggio presents himself as senseless paint, specifically as paint trapped in the body of a man. To support this interpretation, let me conclude by pointing to just one more painting: *The Beheading of St. John*. Notice the old woman standing above the younger woman who is holding the platter. She's looking at the act of beheading and covering her ears, preventing herself from hearing some obscene noise that doesn't seem to bother anyone else. In 1955 and 1956, when this painting was restored, an obtrusive detail came to light. The blood pouring out of St. John's neck turns into Caravaggio's signature. It is the only painting that Caravaggio ever signed.

REFERENCES

Adams, P. (1996). The violence of paint. In *The Emptiness of the Image: Psychoanalysis and Sexual Differences*, pp. 108–121. New York: Routledge.

Bersani, L. (1995). *Homos*. Cambridge, MA: Harvard University Press.

Boyarin, D. (1992). This we know to be the carnal Israel: circumcision and the erotic life of God and Israel. *Critical Inquiry* 18:474–505.

——— (1994). *A Radical Jew: Paul and the Politics of Identity*. Berkeley: University of California Press.

Boyarin, D., and Boyarin, J. (1993). Diaspora: generation and the ground of Jewish identity. *Critical Inquiry* 19:693–725.

Clement, C. (1994). *Syncope: The Philosophy of Rapture*, trans. S. O'Driscoll and D. M. Mahoney. Minneapolis, MN: University of Minneapolis Press.

Copjec, J. (1994). *Read My Desire: Lacan Against the Historicists*. Cambridge, MA: MIT Press.

Dean, T. (1996). Sex and syncope. *Raritan* 15:64–86.

Dolar, M. (1996). The object voice. In *Gaze and Voice as Love Objects*, ed. R. Salecl and S. Zizek, pp. 7–31. Durham, NC: Duke University Press.

Dunand, A. (1990). The end of the treatment. *Newsletter of the Freudian Field* 4:120–133.

Freud, S. (1915). Instincts and their vicissitudes. *Standard Edition* 14:117–140.

——— (1923). *The Ego and the Id. Standard Edition* 19:12–66.

——— (1925). Negation. *Standard Edition* 19:235–239.

——— (1930). *Civilization and its Discontents. Standard Edition* 21:64–145.

———— (1937). Analysis terminable and interminable. *Standard Edition* 23:216–253.

Fried, M. (1997). Thoughts on Caravaggio. *Critical Inquiry* 24:13–57.

Friedlander, W. (1955). *Caravaggio Studies*. Princeton, NJ: Princeton University Press; New York: Schocken, 1969.

Hammill, G. (2000). Being and knowledge: Lacan and the institution of psychoanalysis. *The American Journal of Semiotics* 15 and 16:137–167.

Hibbard, H. (1983). *Caravaggio*. New York: Harper & Row.

Hocquenghem, G. (1993). *Homosexual Desire*, trans. D. Dangoor. Durham, NC: Duke University Press.

Lacan, J. (1955–1956). Seminar III: *The Psychoses*, ed. J-A. Miller, trans. R. Grigg. New York: Norton, 1993.

———— (1959–1960). Seminar VII: *The Ethics of Psychoanalysis*, trans. D. Porter. New York: Norton.

———— (1963–1964). Seminar XI: *The Four Fundamental Concepts of Psychoanalysis*, ed. J-A. Miller, trans. A. Sheridan. New York : Norton, 1977.

———— (1975). Seminar XX: *Encore*, ed. J-A. Miller. Paris: Seuil.

Lupton, J. (1996). *The Afterlives of the Saints: Hagiography, Typology, and Renaissance Literature*. Stanford, CA: Stanford University Press.

Moir, A. (1982). *Caravaggio*. New York: Harry Abrams, 1989.

Sedgwick, E. K. (1993). *Tendencies*. Durham, NC: Duke University Press.

Shepherdson, C. (1994).Vital signs: the place of memory in psychoanalysis. *Research in Phenomenology* 23:61–66.

Zizek, S. (1991). *Looking Awry. An Introduction to Jacques Lacan Through Popular Culture*. Cambridge, MA: MIT Press.

———— (1992). *Enjoy Your Symptom: Jacques Lacan in Hollywood and Out*. New York: Routledge.

4

On Critics, Sublimation, and the Drive: The Photographic Paradoxes of the Subject

Juli Carson

What would a model of the psychic relation between the critic and his object look like, one that relinquished the desire for mastery and openly embraced the manner in which transference-love and narcissism drive the pursuit of a given object? Roland Barthes' later writings (specifically *A Lover's Discourse* [1978] and *Camera Lucida* [1981]) instance the critic's attempt to work himself out of complicity with the materialist, semiotic certitude based upon the academic law of "critical distance" and scientificity. By moving toward a psychoanalytic model in the late work, one that performatively demonstrates the operations of such an approach, Barthes openly embraced and exposed the manner in which the repressed dynamics of narcissism and transference-love constitute the critic's so-called "object of knowledge." In so doing, what his discourse directly takes up is how the operations of the photograph (his object) mirrored that of the subject (the critic). To unpack this problematic, of course, necessitates an examination of what drives Barthes in particular, and the critic in general.

WHOSE ROLAND BARTHES?

Let me begin with an anecdote. In a recent conference on visual studies, a prominent semiotician and art historian argued the necessity of
returning our attention to the materiality of an artwork. The critic's
object of study was a drawing made by Georges Seurat of his mother.
What was absolutely central to the presentation was the critic's alignment of his own subjectivity with that of the artist's, such that in
describing a drawing of the artist's mother, the luminous space under
her chin was said to provide the viewer-critic with a "punctum." This
term, taken from Roland Barthes' *Camera Lucida*, is commonly used
in contemporary discourse to describe the effect of a small detail that
"shoots" out from an image, accidentally "pricking" the subject because the detail signifies something outside the parameters of language. However, what is curious about the use of the term "punctum"
here, in the context of proto-modernist drawing, is that Barthes was
speaking of the punctum explicitly as a *photographic* effect. And yet,
it is the current doxa of *Camera Lucida* to extend the concept of "punctum" to describe any disturbing detail in any given visual medium.
Moreover, the desire to take up Barthes' subject position (that is, the
contemporary critic's desire to *feel* Barthes' punctum in relation to his
own object of study) has supplanted what Barthes' performative discovery of the punctum teaches us about the role of the critic in the first
place.

So, what if we were to return more faithfully to Barthes' concept
of the punctum? In *Camera Lucida*, Barthes sets out to prove that
behind every photograph lies Death, a fact that his text explicates
through a performative of the scopic drive's operations. This performative is initiated by Barthes' alignment with the vectors of the
gaze, apparent in the very first lines when he states—in response to
looking at a photograph of Napoleon's youngest brother, Jerome—"I
am looking at the eyes that looked at the Emperor." This jarring realization—that the corpus of photography circles around the corpse
of the photographed subject—presents the viewer with a subject
indexically caught within the *atemporal* vector of the gaze (*I am looking at someone that at once sees and can no longer do so*). It is in this

instance of an impossible atemporality, one that points us to an undefinable space—what Jacques Lacan called the split between the eye (the imaginary space of vision) and the gaze (a courier from the unrepresentable real)—that Barthes' drive to *know* photography's essence is manifested.

In recent cultural discourse, however, critics have read Barthes' text in relation to the "annihilating" effect that "traumatic" contemporary images have on the viewer. Moreover, critics theorize this effect as being a traumatic "encounter with the real." In support, the unsettling experience Barthes describes in looking at the *details* of certain photographs is emphasized. Most notable on this account is Hal Foster's (1996) *Return of the Real*. However, this approach fundamentally overlooks the manner in which the gaze, if it indeed surfaces in Barthes' text as a courier of the Lacanian real, is *not* located within the identifiable details of a given photograph. Rather it *enters into play* that which the photograph *can't* represent but can only *effect*—that is, the atemporal operation of a subject's drives. And this subject, in Barthes' text, is posited as a metaphor for the critic himself.

Thus said, I want to enter into Barthes' text differently than the two reigning approaches I have provided here. By focusing instead upon the performative aspect of his late work, in which Barthes strategically occupies the position of critic-analysand, a new "site" of analysis is introduced: the personal as endlessly, outwardly expanding, dialectically engaged as it is with the concretized "nonsite" of a concretized public doxa or convention. It was Robert Smithson, of course, who articulated the counterintuitive distinction between "site" and "nonsite," and it is useful to recall in the context of Barthes' project. According to Smithson (1996), a site (a place we go and physically occupy) puts into play "open limits, a series of points, outer coordinates, subtraction, indeterminate certainty, scattered information, reflection, edge, some place (physical), and the many" (pp. 152–153). Inversely, the nonsite (a place within the order of representation) posits "closed limits, an array of matter, inner coordinates, addition, determinate uncertainty, contained information, mirror, center, no place (abstract), and the one" (pp. 152–153).

In the case of Smithson's *Spiral Jetty*, the nonsite may loosely be configured as the work's photographic representation—something locatable that can only be seen at a distance. The site, on the other hand, would be experienced upon arrival at this famous work, at which point the actual jetty (no doubt seen by the traveler first as a point on a map or a photograph in a book) experientially both dissolves and endlessly expands. This is evident by the fact that the traveler can't *see* the jetty from where he *is*. Site and nonsite, however, are inextricably locked together in a *truncated* dialectic, whereby "a double path made up of sign, photographs, and maps . . . belong to both sides of the dialectic at once" (Smithson 1996, pp. 152–153). This problematic is beautifully demonstrated in the cinematic representation of Smithson running along his jetty, captured from the air by helicopter. Here we see the "personal experience" of the subject on site, endlessly expanding, the gestalt experience of the jetty dissolving under his feet. However, our seeing Smithson on film, coupled with Smithson's knowledge that he is performing for the camera, exposes the manner in which the subject's personal experience is caught and therefore always already mediated in advance by the closed limitation of his own photographic representation.

This mediation plays itself out further by the existence of a story board for the film that precedes Smithson's entry into the "site." Moreover, the film itself then becomes another "site" for the viewer to experience—though this site is always already bound up as a nonsite in contrast to Smithson's actual experience of *Jetty* with which we are filmically presented. Lest we not recognize the film's duplicitous signification as both site and nonsite, the last shot of Smithson's film presents us with an aerial photograph of Spiral Jetty tacked to the wall of his studio. The "nonsite" of *Jetty's* secondary representation is further repeated by the spiral form of the reels attached to the film projector positioned in front of the jetty's photographic representation— a signifier of the film itself as "nonsite." Hence, the desire to *locate* which is the site (private experience) and which is the nonsite (public convention), in both *Spiral Jetty's* physical and filmic manifestations, outside of any theoretical dialectic, leads the subject into an infinite regress.[10]

But why introduce such a site—the privatized—into our analysis, especially if it is resistant to being fastened down? Is this just more Dematerialist practice?[11] Not if we begin with the premise that the so-called discrete site of the "personal" is always unknowable outside the nonsite of language, which constitutes the mythic status of the personal. This is where Smithson and Barthes converge, which brings us back to Barthes' investigation of such subjective (photo-

---

10. The manner in which site (place) and nonsite (representation) are bound up together recalls the operation of the drive, which I will return to at length in the epilogue. However, to state the analogy in terms of Smithson's site/nonsite briefly here, we can think of Smithson's dialectic alongside the operations of the drive's two main components: the life drive (Eros) and the death drive (Thanatos), figured by Freud as bound and unbound energies, respectively. The bound energy (representation) points us to the secondary process (preconscious) where unbound free-flowing or contradictory energy (of the unconscious) is experienced by the subject as a compromised pleasure in the state of word or image-units (consciousness). These two energies of Eros (form) and Thanatos (entropy), thought here, again along the lines of nonsite and site, are contradictory but not dialectical because they are not reconciled into a stable third term. That is to say, there is no cause (thesis) and an effect (antithesis), or a ground upon which a contradiction is waged and further reconciled. Rather, in a more Lacanian read of the drive, Slavoj Zizek (1996) has said of the two:

> ". . . Eros and Thanatos or expansion and contradiction as the opposed forces [are] engaged in an unending and unrelenting battle for domination. The co-dependence of the two antagonistic forces [thus] does not reside in the fact that one force needs the other as the only ground against which it can assert itself. . . ." [p. 28]

11. Dematerialist practice, a branch of seventies Conceptualism, is best represented by the work of Douglas Huebler and Robert Barry. Doing away with the actual art object in place of a given mental proposition, the Dematerialists were deeply concerned with discrete privatized spaces, as their motto "live in your head" testified. Contemporaneous with this movement, Jack Burnham's (1970) essay "Alice's Head: Reflections on Conceptual Art" thus described the Dematerialists' ideal medium as "telepathy." For a critique of the inherent Cartesian element of such strategies, see Rosalind Krauss's (1973) "Sense and Sensibility."

graphic) paradoxes. It is important to note at the start, however, that the roots for Barthes' analysis of the *atopic* site of the personal (in his late writings) already lies in his early investigation of photography's paradoxical status, explicated (nonperformatively) in his series of articles, "The Photographic Message," "Rhetoric of the Image," and "The Third Meaning." For it is in these essays that a pivot can be located between Barthes' early structuralist Marxist work, in which the critic stood (dialectically) outside the investigation of his chosen object of analysis, and his late psychoanalytic investigations, in which the object of analysis is *necessarily* read through the (nondialectical) paradoxical site of the critic-analysand. Though the performative analysis is yet to be enacted in these early essays, what is nevertheless interesting is the manner in which a foundation is laid for an understanding of the analogy between subject and photograph.

THE PHOTOGRAPH-AS-SUBJECT

In "The Photographic Message," a photographic paradox is established around the impossible site of *pure* denotation—the "thing-in-itself" in psychoanalytic terms. Quite simply, the photograph, as that "message without a code," can only signify as such *through* the cultural myth of photography's own naturalness. This is the contradiction at work in the subject whose feeling of "denotation" or "analogical plenitude" in front of the photograph is so great that the photograph's description is "literally impossible." For to *describe* "consists precisely in joining to the denoted message a relay or second-order message derived from a code which is that of language and constituting in relation to the photographic analogue . . . a connotation" (Barthes 1977a, pp. 18–19). Yet this belief in a photograph's analogical plenitude is, itself, always already the photograph's own description. Thus, photographic denotation alone, pure indexicality, is impossible. And by extension, the subject—analogous to photographic denotation—can never be that "thing-in-itself" within language. That is, the subject can't exist *outside* of its compromised state within language, though it is continually driven to do so. And fantasy, or desire, is the *narrative* that circles around this primordial loss.[12]

It is thus the perceived loss of a primordial status of pureness or wholeness in the face of language that drives both the subject's general desire for partial objects in the world and the subject's specific uncanny relation to photography's paradoxical status. In this way, *every* photograph is a self-portrait for the subject, as in both the subject and the photograph, an unnamable "reality" drives a consciously *perceived* loss of its pure (preconnotative) status. But such a lost state (or object) is always, like denotation, traumatically situated outside of language. Thus, trauma can't be *pictured as a detail*, but only put into operation as that which circles *around* language, *driving* it as it were. "The Photographic Message" explicitly makes this connection, which will be played out more fully in *Camera Lucida*. For it is in this earlier essay that we already find Barthes musing as to whether a pure denotative, or a "this-side of language," is impossible. To which he asserts that "if such denotation exists, it is perhaps not at the level of

---

12. In his essay "Suture," Jacques-Alain Miller (1977–1978) demonstrates, through recourse to Gotlobb Frege's *Foundations of Arithmetic*, how the subject is subsumed into language as a "thing-not-itself." Miller mathematically theorized the concept of suture in relation to a nonrepresentable "lack"—one that constitutes the subject inasmuch as the subject constitutes lack. The subject itself, therefore, may be that which is lacking, but its lack exists in the form of a "stand-in."

Frege asserts that every number is defined by its predecessor, such that the infinite set of numbers is reduced "to the number one and increased by one, [such that] every one of the infinitely numeral formulae can be probed from a few general propositions." In turn, Miller states that what is logically specific to Frege's system "is that each concept is only defined and exists solely through the relation which it maintains as subsumer with that which it subsumes." For instance, the object (in this case the actual instance of nothing before the chain of numbers) exists only by falling under the concept (the marker "zero" within the chain of numbers). From the zero (nothing) to the "zero" (a number), a lack, or a gap, is rendered visible between the thing "in-itself" and an object "not-identical-with-itself." Like the subject who is named upon entering language, "the zero, understood as a number which assigns to the subsuming concept the lack of an object, is as such a thing—the first non-real thing in thought." Analogously, we can see this as the impossibility of pure photographic denotation.

what ordinary language calls the insignificant, the neutral, the objective, but on the contrary, at the level of absolutely traumatic images" (Barthes 1977a, p. 30). Such that an absolutely traumatic image, as pure denotation, would indeed *be* traumatic not because it meant something awful, but because it meant nothing at all. Which is to say, it would point to a primordial *loss of being* (rather than wholeness) under the heel of total linguistic suspension.

In "Rhetoric of the Image," the temporal aspect of this loss is played out through another aspect of the photographic paradox: the gap between a photograph's denotative reality (the *then-there*) and its spatial immediacy to the subject (the *here-now*). Whereas the first photographic paradox hinges on the *reality* of a thing in the world, this second paradox hinges on that thing's *temporal position* within the world, such that on the denotative level, although the photograph is full of symbols, ". . . there nonetheless remains in the photograph, insofar as the literal message is sufficient, a kind of natural *being-there* of the objects: nature seems spontaneously to produce the scene represented" (Barthes 1977a, p. 45). Yet, as with denotation that can signify only through connotation, the photograph's temporal status as having "been-there" can only be known through the subject's ascertaining of it in the "here-now." And as in the first photographic paradox, this second temporal paradox mirrors the subject's own atemporal problematic. This is the foundation of a psychoanalytic understanding of the subject, which Freud (1899) describes in "Screen Memories." In response to the question, "Do we have *any* memories at all from our childhood?" Freud asserts that we only have memories *related* to our childhood. Which is to say, the nature of childhood memories, the manner in which they suddenly appear and disappear in simultaneous modes and forms, demonstrates that one's earliest years are never experienced *as they were*. Rather, these past moments are paradoxically experienced in the present, triggered by related events taking place at the time of the memory's (present) formation. As Freud (1899) puts it, "In these periods of revival, the childhood memories did not, as people are accustomed to say, 'emerge.' They were 'formed' at that time" (p. 69).

Counter to this, a linear concept of time—one in which a narrative progresses unidirectionally from beginning to end—is what predicates a conventional materialist model of history. In his essay "The Third Meaning," it was such a unilateral model that Barthes sought to rupture through his explication of an "obtuse" element in film (and language). Like Bataille's notion of the *informe*, to which Barthes refers in this essay, the obtuse meaning provides " . . . a multi-layering of meanings which always lets the previous meaning continue, as in a geological formation, saying the opposite without giving up the contrary" (Barthes 1977a, pp. 60–61). As such, the obtuse meaning isn't a developmental language system; rather it slips in between the progressive dialectical terms upon which language is founded. The obtuse meaning in narrative film finds itself in the "filmic" quality of the displaced film *still*—that counternarrative signifying nothing on its own in relation to any particular narrative, but which nevertheless relies on that narrative to define that which it *exceeds*. And if it exceeds narrativity, which is to say language, it does so individually, never collectively.

This, of course, is a clear inference to Lacan's notion of an unrepresentable "real," demonstrated by Barthes' ability to signify the obtuse meaning only through its *effect*. As such, the third meaning (the obtuse meaning) is "theoretically locatable but not describable" as "it begins where metanarrative ends." And yet, paradoxically, the image's obtuse meaning (as that *nonrepressed* meaning) needs to be situated *within* language in order to exceed it. This nonrepressed, inarticulable element in film, again, points to a site of an operationally present but unnamable trauma upon which subjectivity, in psychoanalytic terms, is founded.[13]

Thus there are three paradoxes that constitute the photograph: the message without a code that can be known therefore only *as a*

---

13. Again, Miller's account of the subject is relevant here. The subject's exclusion from the discourse with which he is paradoxically bound up is what Miller ultimately calls suture. Rather than a "suturing" that *mends* a wound, Miller's account of it *initiates* one. This phantasmatically missing element, which constitutes the wound in the subject as he enters language, is located in the real. As such, this perceived lack necessarily can't enter into language (representation), though it is what *drives* the subject within it.

code, the denotation of a natural past that can only be known vis-à-vis a *cultural present*, and a nonrepressed meaning only known *as meaning* within language. If these photographic paradoxes are the same as the paradoxes of the subject, as I have argued, how then could Barthes *not* address the subject as that element imbricated in the critic's analysis of photography? Which is to say, how could he extricate *himself* from this analysis? Considering the subject's fascination with photography's operation (as a mirror of the self), to separate the critic's subjective position from an analysis of the photograph would be to comply (uncritically) with the narcissistic impulse of the analysis at hand. For if the operations of narcissism are that the subject loves *what he himself is, was, would like to be, or was once a part of him*, does this not also describe the relation of the subject to the photograph, and by extension the critic to his object of study—photography?

THE OBSCENE CRITIC

It is precisely this narcissistic relation between the critic and his object, a form of transference-love, that Barthes argues *must* be put under analysis in his subsequent essay "Writers, Intellectuals, Teachers." This means that it is not just the *object* of a critic's study that must be analyzed, but simultaneously the critic's subjective construction *around* it. If the previous essays discussed the paradoxes of photography, "Writers" takes up the paradox of speech as it relates to those who use it and thus are defined by it: specifically, the teacher. The teacher's dilemma—for it is he who speaks—circles around his inability to maintain authority within a medium (speech) that by its nature disprivileges its user (the speaker). Barthes (1977a) states:

> Imagine that I am a teacher: I speak, endlessly, in front of and for someone who remains silent. I am the person who says "I," I am the person who, under cover of setting out a body of knowledge, puts out a discourse, never knowing how that discourse is being received and thus forever forbidden the reassurance of a definitive image—even if offensive—which would constitute me. [p. 194]

From this dilemma comes what Barthes (1977a) calls the "odor of speech": the "dizzying turn of the image: one exalts or regrets what one has said, the way in which one has said it, one *imagines oneself* (turns oneself over in an image)" (p. 204). This, again, relates to the critic-teacher posited here as the analysand: he who speaks to a silent other in which he locates the authenticity of his desire. In *A Lover's Discourse*, the notion of the teacher-analysand is taken further to allegorically position the critic-analysand within the hysterical state of being in love. In both texts, there is a turn away from a structuralist position of critical distance, which Barthes had previously taken vis-à-vis his object of analysis. The blind spot of such "critical-distance" models is the presumption that a given doxa automatically has political viability. Barthes, in fact, argued that these models merely repeated the symbolic Law-of-the-Father in the guise of "scientificity." Instead, Barthes argues for a playful "para-doxa,"[14] allowing him alternatively to play the "bad" teacher or critic in "Writers" and *Lover's Discourse*, one who willfully transfers authority onto his object of study, flaunting his narcissistic identification with it, and openly loving that which he *wants to be*. The premise in doing so is that such transference is, in fact, what really *constitutes* "objective" writing, though that which constitutes it is necessarily *repressed*.

In his final work, *Camera Lucida*, the performativity argued for in "Writers" and enacted in *Lover's Discourse* is put into play via his return to the photographic paradoxes explicated in his earlier essays. And if the critic's relation to his object is theorized implicitly along the operations of the drive in previous texts,[15] this relation is conceptually and structurally foundational to understanding the critic's position within *Camera Lucida*. For here, in *Camera Lucida*, we circle

---

14. In *Roland Barthes by Roland Barthes* (1977b), "para-doxa" is defined as a move from the doxa of political writing based upon popular opinion, to a critique of the writer's desire within the space of writing.

15. I am referring to the manner in which both the subject is driven to retrieve a phantasmatically "lost" object (Miller, 1977–1978) and representation is inextricably bound up with what is "outside" it. Both these operatations are analogous to the three photographic paradoxes defined by Barthes.

back around to that obscene object of materialist, critical study: the personal, the subjective, the private. But it was such an atopic discourse of the personal, theorized around the state of *jouissance*, that Barthes argued to be *the last site* of political engagement at the pre sumed "end of history." Thus if the Left's complicity with metahistory, positivism, and scientificity foundered it in hegemonic doxa, the anachronistic and obscene nature of the privatized subject (the critic as analysand or Lover) held a disruptive appeal for Barthes, which he clearly stated in *Lover's Discourse*:

> Whatever is anachronistic is obscene. As a (modern) divinity History is repressive, History forbids us to be out of time. Of the past we tolerate only ruin, the monument, kitsch, what is amusing: we reduce this past to no more than its signature. The lover's sentiment is old-fashioned, but his antiquation cannot even be recuperated as a spectacle: love falls outside of interesting time; no historical polemical meaning can be given it; it is this that is obscene. [Barthes 1978, p. 178]

Now, this interest in the obscene disruption of history's repressive mechanism is what leads Barthes to take up a performative analysis of the privatized space of viewing in *Camera Lucida*. From this space, Barthes theorizes the "quality of photography as an element that society continually tames via the tyranny of the spectacle" (implicitly put forth by Barthes in Debordian terms).[16] He also openly exposes the manner in which his own subject position, previously repressed,

---

16. In *Society of the Spectacle*, Guy Debord's (1994) subjectivity is defined by a perceived loss of "real lived experience" in the face of an all-consuming spectacle culture. Debord argues that the spectacle, a social relationship between people mediated by images, offers us a false sense of unity: "Images detached from every aspect of life merge into a common stream, and the former unity of life is lost forever" (p. 12). Debord, by naively longing for a prior state of unity or wholeness, is intuiting the dilemma of the subject's suture into representation. As the neurotic subject, he believed in the possibility of returning to such a state of pure-lived "completeness." Barthes, informed by Lacanian discourse, is more ambivalent about this. Rather than arguing that we can get there (for there is no "there" there), Barthes performs the subject's desire to do so, critically "enjoying his symptom," in Slavoj Zizek's terms.

is actually constitutive of any "scientific" inquiry into photography's so-called "ontology."

"DRIVING" *CAMERA LUCIDA*

What does it mean to put "the drive" back into *Camera Lucida*? Simply, it repositions Barthes' site of analysis, which is to say, his object of study. Late in my graduate studies I enrolled in independent studies with my thesis advisor to study Barthes' late writings. My advisor, having previously studied Barthes within the context of the Frankfurt School, had conducted only a polemical reading of this material prior to our meeting. Nevertheless, he was pleased to return to this work within the framework of a materialist understanding of queer theory, to which he had recently been exposed. And there we sat, face to face, *Camera Lucida* in hand, poring over what he saw as the writings of a structuralist turned "mama's boy." Then came his admission of the Left's reaction-formation vis-à-vis the late Roland Barthes: "When Barthes published this work, after his earlier political writings, we Marxists indignantly asked, 'Is this what politics, history itself, comes down to? The story of *a boy and his mother?*'" To this I simply replied, "Yes." Finally, at the end of our session, the dismissal of that which Marxists held to be the most obscene was uttered: "I mean, we thought, 'This is a turn toward privatization!'"

Years later I realized what my advisor couldn't see: that *he* occupied Barthes' site of analysis. This blind spot—the unconscious, paradoxical desire to be *outside* of language in order to escape its odorous, annihilating effect—is *precisely* the object of Barthes' late writings, concluding with *Camera Lucida*. Ironically, other critics who have not dismissed *Camera Lucida* have redeemed it through the "scientificity" of its main principles: the "studium" and "punctum." However, rather than being seduced into the use-value of these concepts as a form of metacritique, we need to ask why and how these elements were put into play to begin with.

In search of a method to describe what strikes him when "looking at the eyes that looked at the emperor," Barthes admits his discomfort in being a subject torn between two languages—the expressive and the critical. To know photography's essence, then, is to step into this space between criticality and expressivity, to know it phenomenologically. It is at this point, as Barthes decides to look only at work that has an effect upon *him*, that the critic's position and that of his object become conflated. First, the admission that feeling oneself observed by the lens makes him both an object and subject: "The photograph," he says, "is the advent of myself as other."

To be photographed, then, is to return to the horror side of Lacan's mirror stage: that moment whereupon the subject, seeing his double in the mirror, is neither subject nor object, but a noncoalesced subject who feels the threat of *becoming* an object. Photographed, he is caught, fractured, fixed into this doubled, objectified state in which (like a photograph) he is neither here nor there:

> In front of the lens, I am at the same time: the one I think I am, the one I want others to think I am, the one the photographer thinks I am, and the one he makes use of to exhibit his art. In other words, a strange action: I do not stop imitating myself, and because of this, each time I am (or let myself be) photographed, I invariably suffer from a sensation of inauthenticity, sometimes imposture (comparable to certain nightmares). [Barthes 1981, p. 13]

What saves him, driving him forward away from this scopic mortification, is the clicking sound created by the photographer's finger, which triggers the lens and thus the metallic shifting of the plates. For Barthes this is the very sound of time's *forward* motion. That is to say, it is the physical, pulsating sound of the drive (one frame after another) that represses what each singular photograph simultaneously initiates at any given point in the photographic session—the subject's *return* to death.[17]

---

17. Here I am again referring to the Drive as theorized by Freud (1920) in "Beyond the Pleasure Principle." Jean Laplanche (1976) extends the paradox of masochistic pleasure/unpleasure implicit in Freud's text, in order to describe an individual divided within himself and against himself. Laplanche describes the paradox this way: ". . . one of the agencies of (the superego) derives its pleasure *from the very fact* of inflicting unpleasure on another agency (the ego). . . . If, in the sa-

Soon after this, Barthes describes a similar anxiety effected by looking at photographs in general. Sometimes in addition to the numbing effect of connotation (the studium), an inexplicable detail triggers a feeling of vertigo in the subject (the punctum). In recent writing, it has been misunderstood that a studium alone signifies something "that-has-been" versus the punctum's effect, which is thought to cut across this denotative field. However, Barthes is clear to continue his early theorizations of the photograph as that which *always* signifies a *thing has been there*. It is important to note, then, that both the studium and the punctum stem from the subject's realization that something "has-been" in the photograph, though the studium tames the effect such a realization has on the subject while the punctum agitates it.

In part one of *Camera Lucida*, he identifies this punctum with an accidental detail in a photograph, caught there without the photographer's intention, which "works" on him. For instance, he sees the punctum at work in the strapped pumps of a black woman or the huge Danton collar of a retarded boy. But, like trauma or the obtuse meaning, the punctum is unnamable, endlessly, metonymically expanding. Thus once Barthes identifies a punctum in a given detail (a partial object, as it were), he later realizes he was *actually* struck by something else and moves on:

> Reading Van der Zee's photograph, I thought I had discerned what moved me: the strapped pumps of the black woman in her Sunday best; but this photograph has worked within me, and later on

---

distic scenario, the pleasure is in the subject and the unpleasure in the object, the introjection of the latter and its integration into an agency of the personality (the ego) would result in an *internalization of the entire scene*, thus accounting at minimal expense for the paradox of masochism; the masochist would achieve enjoyment only through his fantasmatic identification with the active pole of the scene" (p. 104). We can extend the manner in which the subject internalizes the primal scene of castration—the loss of the thing-in-itself—to Barthes' masochistic experience of the photographic session. Barthes, as that subject divided within himself and against himself, derives satisfactory pleasure at the forward sound of the camera's clicking insofar as it affords the paradoxical, frenetic, and sadistic pleasure of the loss of a coalesced "self" vis-à-vis his photographic representation (i.e., his mortification).

> I realized that the real punctum was the necklace (a slender rib-
> bon of braided gold) which I had seen worn by someone in my
> own family, and which, once she died, remained shut up in a family
> box of old jewelry. . . . I realized that however immediate and in-
> cisive it was, the punctum could accommodate a certain latency
> (but never any scrutiny). [Barthes 1981, p. 53]

In part two, when he looks at photographs of his recently deceased
mother, this latent quality of the punctum is further played out. It is
no longer locatable in a given detail alone but in the photograph's
atemporal status, which mirrors that of the subject, hence the reason
that the subject is simultaneously so fascinated and disturbed by the
photograph. Barthes explicates this through a strategically performed
autobiographical account, stemming from a search for his mother's
"air" among a pile of images from her dresser drawer.

AUTOBIOGRAPHY-AS-SITE

"One November evening shortly after my mother's death, I was going
through some photographs," Barthes (1981) begins, only to discover
that none of them seemed "right" (p. 63). Rather than her image, it is
the supplemental objects within the photograph that he associates with
her. That element of the photograph distinguishing it from a drawing—the overall nature of denoting something that wasn't intentionally photographed—becomes the "truth" of the photograph. And in
this insistence, he finds the "truth" of his mother. Driven by a melancholic pursuit of his mother's lost "being," he thus finds his mother
displaced in the objects that he has a strong cathexis to—the "rumpled
softness of her crepe de Chine," for instance. Again, the detail as partial object is where Barthes first locates his punctum.

But then comes the realization that these objects need to be repeatedly discovered, in order to keep her being *by proxy*. He dreams
about her, Barthes says, but he does not dream *her*. "And confronted
with the photograph, as in the dream, it is the same effort, the same
Sisyphean labor: to reascend, straining toward the essence, to climb back
down without having seen it, and to begin all over again" (p. 66). But

he, the critic—at once also in the position of the son-lover—is not consciously in control of this pursuit. As she provides his *objet a* (his object cause of desire) in the guise of a lost being, she, unlike him, is perceived as being more in control of her image. She, as the other in the maternal dyad, the subject supposed to know, the subject in whom he finds meaning but from whom he is consequently alienated, lends herself to the photograph the way he can't. And then finally, amid the images at hand, he "finds" her, not in the denoted guise of his own mother, but in the image of his mother as a little girl in the Winter Garden. It is here that he not only finds her "air"—in the "sovereign Good of childhood"—but it is also the "moment that everything turned around," when he "discovered her *as into herself*" (p. 71). And it is at this moment that the mother, whom he had nursed on her deathbed in a primordial return to the original dyad, becomes *his* little girl.

The "truth" of the punctum, after all, was *not* in the singular detail but in the stunning reversal of temporal roles, the moment in which the drive's contrary impulse toward life and death displays itself along the atemporal vectors of a moebius strip. And this, Barthes concludes, is the real essence of photography: the moment that a punctum exposes to light an anterior future, working on us because it allows for a certain repressed recursivity of the subject to be exposed.[18] He tests

---

18. Again, we can conceive of this atemporality along the paradox of masochism, inherent in the death drive, as described by Laplanche (1976). For such a paradox has an atemporal relation to trauma much like the photographic paradoxes that Barthes describes. Laplanche states of this "paradoxical pleasure" that there is a confusion of which way the subject is driven—toward growth or entropy. Moreover, to pick growth (Eros) is to move the subject paradoxically on to death, to pick entropy (Thanatos) is to move us closer to our own birth. Ultimately, what the subject wants is out of this paradox, out of the very pressures of the drive. Laplanche states: "At stake then is an effort to grasp what is most 'driven' in the drive—ataraxy, Nirvana as the abolition of every drive—and what is most vital in the biological—death, explicitly designated as the 'final aim' of life" (p. 107). In Barthes' text, however, such a flight is not taken through the usual sublimation tactics. Rather, the masochistic impulse to locate the subject's paradox (vis-à-vis the same formative paradox within the photograph) is painfully played out. Admittedly, this is achieved through discourse; thus there is a secondary sublimation at play. However, if it is possible to have an encounter with the Real, this would be the location of that pulse within Barthes' text—*not* in any given detail.

this discovery on other images, and finds it operates in all photographs in which time, "the lacerating emphasis of the *noeme* (that-has-been)," becomes pure representation. In looking at a photograph of Lewis Payne on death row (for trying to assassinate Secretary of State W. H. Seward in 1865), he described the photograph precisely in terms of a drive consisting of contradictory movements:

> The photograph is handsome, as is the boy: that is the studium. But the punctum is: "He is going to die." I read at the same time: "This will be" and "This has been." I observe with horror an anterior future of which death is the stake. By giving me the absolute past of the pose (aorist), the photograph tells me death in the future. What "pricks" me is the discovery of this equivalence. In front of the photograph of my mother as a child, I tell myself: she is going to die: I shudder like Winnicott's psychotic patient, over a catastrophe which has already occurred. Whether the subject is already dead, every photograph is this catastrophe. [Barthes 1981, p. 96]

This "death in the future" recalls the main component of the pleasure principle, through which Freud (1926) describes the main (repressed) operation of the drive: that the ultimate goal of life is death. Again, Freud reminds us that the goal of life is not "a state of things which have never been attained," but a general moving *forward*. He states clearly that it "must be an old state of things, an initial state from which the living entity has at one time or other departed and to which it is striving to return by the circuitous paths along which its development leads" (p. 38).[19] It is precisely *this* moment, in both the subject and the photograph, that the Winter Garden and Lewis Payne photographs expose in the form of the atemporal "punctum."

Such a photographic-subjective operation could only be exposed performatively by Barthes, by putting *himself* in the picture, so to speak, first as a photographed subject in part one and second as the melancholic subject in part two. The repression of such an autobiographic impulse of scientific "discovery" was precisely what charac-

---

19. This desire to return to a lost state also repeats Miller's explication of the subject's desire to retain a phantasmatically "lost" object.

terized, what actually *constituted*, according to Jacques Derrida (1987), Freud's discovery of the pleasure principle and hence the drive. For the discovery of the fort-da game (the child throwing a spool in the corner of the room and repetitively retrieving it in order to "master" the loss of the mother through this surrogate) is not a scientific observation. Rather it signifies the grandfather-observer (the analyst), Derrida argues, *as* a participant in his *own* game of fort-da.

Freud (1920) himself reflects upon his discovery of the fort-da game that "it was more than a fleeting observation, for I lived under the same roof as the child and his parents for some weeks . . ." (p. 14). Remarkably, this child is not any child, but the child of Freud's recently deceased daughter. Such being the case, Derrida theorizes that the melancholic impulses behind Freud's scientific discovery provide an accidental autobiographic discovery, whereby the same stunning chronological reversal unwittingly occurs in Freud's text as it intentionally did in Barthes' narrative. The grandfather *becomes* the grandson, and the fort-da game Freud's performative reaction to the loss of his own "legacy":

> He the grandson of his grandfather, the grandfather of the grandson, compulsively repeats repetition [in his discovery of the drive] without going anywhere. . . . In question is not only a folding back or tautological reversal, as if the grandson, by offering the mirror of his writing, were in advance dictating to what he had to set down on paper. . . . [Derrida 1987, p. 303]

This "tautological" impulse does not discredit the discovery of the drive, as one reading of the Derrida text might have us believe. Instead, it relocates the site of discovery, for rather than Freud discovering the drive in this repressed autobiographical site, the drive (like the purloined letter) finds *him*.[20]

Now, what if we were to favor a critical strategy of discovery that *openly displayed* the psycho-phenomenological[21] nature of the critic's autobiographic relation to his object of knowledge? Which is to say, what if the critic were not to feign ignorance of his subjective position in the process of analysis? This, I have argued, is precisely the

---

20. Further elaboration is useful here, as Derrida's text directly relates to Barthes' project. "Freud's Legacy" unpacks the performative nature of repetition compulsion that unconsciously attends Freud's traumatic loss of his legacy, which in turn writes itself *into* (through) "Beyond the Pleasure Principle." This "loss" is bound up with the aporic status of the name in relation to Freud's family lineage as well as to his own science, his name being "gone" in the very space of its presence as a sign. This occurs in two ways: (1) in the child-legacy (*gone* is the family name, but *there* is the boy), and (2) in the father of psychoanalysis (*gone* is his name in place of scientific results, *there* is the science "of" his own name). This, in fact, is what "drives" Freud's text, and it is also what the text subsequently shows us against its author's intentions. "Beyond the Pleasure Principle" isn't *about* repetition compulsion and the death drive, anecdotally described through the game of fort-da. Rather, it is a de-monstration of fort-da in relation to Freud's own drive. Derrida thus describes Freud's essay in terms of an "orphaned" text that performs (itself) what it means to describe: "It is auto-bio-thanato-hetero-graphic scene of writing. . . . This scene does not recount something, the content of an event which would be called fort-da. This remains unrepresentable, but produces, producing itself, the scene of writing" (p. 332).

21. This is not an oxymoron, as the partial objects, which we know through our body's spatial relation to them, stem from a mental cathexis.

means through which Barthes cut through the unconscious narcissistic tendency of the materialist critic in relation to his object. The purpose of doing so, as I have also argued, had a quasi-Situationist component; by relating the operations of the photograph to that of the subject, an image could be "experienced" outside the deadening, tyrannical spectacle of commodity consumption. I have not tested the validity of this political conclusion, for it is not the intention of this paper to do so. Rather, I have intended to *locate* a political component in the (politically obscene) turn toward the lyrically personal in Barthes' late work. Such an observation allows for an understanding of *Camera Lucida* not as a scientific text on photography but as a theoretical text that makes *use* of photographic analysis. This it does as a means of defining a critical model of autobiographic performativity—one that addresses the critic's complicity with the very doxa he seeks to undermine. Simply put, it is a means of "interrogating the interrogation."[22]

EPILOGUE

A final anecdote: Last year, I was asked to write an essay on Renée Green's (1997) project "Partially Buried" for a retrospective exhibition of her work at the Secession in Vienna. I was expected ostensibly to write an essay positioning Green's work within the history of Conceptualist practice, as that was my specialty, having completed a similar piece on Mary Kelly for the Generali Foundation, also in Vienna. In the Kelly piece, I had imbricated the voice of the analyst-archivist with the work's explication, such that the archivist's "desire to know" Kelly's work openly constituted the parameters of my investigation. For the Green piece, I took this even farther, opting for a critical, lyrical response to the signifiers of race that Green's work cast off for the viewer to see and thus "know." In short, I answered Derrida's call to Freud, which Barthes implicitly answers in *Camera*

---

22. This is a phrase coined by Mary Kelly, who also took up a model of critical, autobiographic performativity in her work *Post-Partum Document* (see Carson 1998).

Lucida. By refusing to play the analyst-historian alone, I admitted (implicitly by aligning my analysis with the subject's desire to *see* race) that the meaning of Green's work was always already located in the para-doxa of my writing as a *pursuit*.

The piece, of course, was rejected since it exposed a repressed desire of the critic-analyst. Frantz Fanon (1952) has argued that "the fact of blackness" in actuality stems from that fact that "the glances of the other" fix him in the sense that "a chemical solution is fixed by a dye" (p. 109). This fixed subject, photo-graphed by and for the other, is what constitutes a repressed desire for the raced subject's "reality" in contemporary critical discourse. Understood in Fanon's theorizations and Barthes' methodology, "Partially Buried" thus puts Green into operation as both the object *pursued* by the viewer-critic and the subject performatively *in* pursuit of her own "reality." In my essay, reproduced here as a coda, I thus leave the medium of photography but not without the lesson Barthes taught through his exploration of it: that the critic's unconscious drive to *see* his object is inextricably tied to—if not constitutive of—his conscious desire to *know* the object.

Looking for Renée

The film *Bulworth* opens with the eponymous protagonist—a liberal senator whose career began in the Civil Rights Movement—crushed by melancholia over the loss of uncompromised political conviction. Against a wall displaying pictures of the senator working with leading activists from the seventies, the man sits, drink in one hand, head in the other, weeping. A knock on the door reveals a hit man hired by the suicidal Bulworth to kill him sometime during his weekend fundraiser in Los Angeles. Delirious with booze and mania, he becomes a somnambulist, caught somewhere between sleep and consciousness—in that traumatic nonstate Jacques Lacan called the "real." It is in this state that Bulworth—a white, wealthy, middle-aged man amid working-class blacks—begins to speak the impossible. Through a ridiculous mimesis that takes the form of a continual rap song, he begins to speak "race" itself. But of course, this isn't him speaking at all; rather, it is the *Other* that he *speaks*.

For it is in this register of the unspeakable, unrepresentable "real," the site of unrepressed trauma, that race speaks. In the waking world of discourse and representation, the site of inexorably repressed trauma, race is only ever *spoken* in absentia. Race, of course, is exactly what Frantz Fanon tried to speak but couldn't, knowing that the black man was always already spoken by the Other who had discursively woven him "out of a thousand details, anecdotes, and stories" (p. 111). His alienated subjectivity, then, was sutured via a perceived loss of a "Negro past" that barred Fanon from pure "Negrohood"—that phantasmatically lost space of transcendent, precolonial intraraciality. In search of this lost object, the ontological "fact of blackness" (p. 109), Fanon wanders from discursive site to site—from whiteness to negritude—discovering that the *fact* of blackness can only be spoken by the Other, in whom he finds meaning but from whom he is alienated.

In the face of a "real" race forever lost, but paradoxically stuck to him (by proxy) via his "epidermal schema" (pp. 111, 140), like Bulworth, Fanon weeps. *Black Skin, White Masks*, in which Fanon describes his experience, was written in 1952, on the eve of a civil rights movement that tried to reinstate the fact of blackness. Yet, this "fact" is none other than what Renée Green allegorically calls a "non-site" in "Partially Buried." As we know, non-site was the term Robert Smithson (1996) used to designate a closed point of limitation, one that simultaneously points to a site through effacing it. A site, on the other hand, is an expansive, seemingly limitless area within which a particular point is impossible to locate or represent. Transposed to race, "identity"— the collusion of the subject around the "fact" of blackness—is an instance of the non-site. It points to something expansive, but only by expunging it. On the other hand, should race be thought of in terms of an unrepresentable "real," it can be seen as an instance of the site—always unobtainable, but infinitely approachable. It is what drives us to posit, phantasmatically, the Other as the subject supposed to *know* about this thing called blackness. But in ascribing blackness onto a person or cultural space, such "knowledge" is fleeting, merely producing in its place a *non-site*.

It is a mistake to assume that the one driven to "know" the site of race, however, is only the white Other. For it is what drives Green, like Fanon before her. However, her quest is not a melancholic pursuit to retrieve an essential identity; rather it is a performative demonstration of how such a pursuit *constitutes* a series of endlessly shifting, *limitless* identities that change upon encounters or "contact" with the Other. Sometimes upon such contact the Other "presumes too much" of Green, but sometimes Green knowingly presumes too much of the *big* Other—that is to say, the site of history mediated by memory. "Partially Buried" wages an interrogation of this presumption (the Other of Green and Green of the Other) through the act of wandering as an instance of the drive.

In "Partially Buried" this wandering takes us to Kent State, where Green is filmed looking for Smithson's now demolished *Partially Buried Woodshed*. Yet Green's goal is not so external. There is no exclamation, "There it is!" Rather, the *trajectory* of Green's aim is mapped through the installation of videotaped interviews with Smithson's colleagues and photographs of her searching for something she knows no longer exists, but which nevertheless is the object-cause of her desire. But we should be careful not to overdetermine Smithson's work as the *actual* object of pursuit. As a "site" his demolished piece expands, allegorically putting into action a series of trajectories mediated by Green's traumatic memory of the Kent State massacre of May 4, 1970, a riot that Green watched on television without knowing her mother's whereabouts. It is through this "screen" memory that a number of other sites are therefore produced: seventies idealism, maternity, and by extension Green's race itself. These sites may represent objects forever lost, but as lost objects their presence *insists*, constituting the subject because such loss is what drives us. In pursuit of these expansive sites, we may stop at various points of identity—the non-site—around which political action is mobilized, as Green reminds us. But the site—be it of race or gender—is in the register of the drive that *leads* us to these non-sites. In the video, when Green finally locates a remnant of *Partially Buried Woodshed* she pauses, and then moves on with her search.

Green's exhibition at the Secession presents other instances of this search: "gender" and "authorship" are the sites of *Some Chance Operations*, "home" the site of *Flow*, and "nationality" the site of *Tracing Lusitania*. However, while each project documents Green's drive vis-à-vis its respective site, the Secession installation restages this drive through which the *viewer's* object-cause of desire comes to be Green herself. But Green is elusive; one wanders through the labyrinth she provides in pursuit of her—stopping at various (non)sites at which she has provided us something, an index of her presence in the form of an object documenting her own search. They are pieces of her cast off into the world, giving us something to see. But what *is* it that we see?

In "What is a Picture?" Lacan (1963–1964) asks, "If a bird were to paint would it not be by letting fall its feathers, a snake by casting off its scales, a tree by letting fall its leaves?" (p. 114). These little marks, what Lacan called the *objet petit a*, are the things one drops of oneself into the world in order to be a subject forever desiring their irretrievable return. For the fictitious character Bulworth this lost object was political idealism, while for Fanon it was his Negrohood. For Green it is identity produced by such legacies. This "letting fall," then, is a sovereign act because it manifests a drive for a lost object that we necessarily can't *see*. Thus, when Green lets drop these little pieces of her, the drive's site is rendered obsolete or inoperable, becoming a non-site. Still, their limitation is the point at which they expand, piquing our desire, urging us to move along to the next site. Which is to say, they put into operation our drive to know the site of the Other—Green herself—the one we presume too much of, the one in which our object-cause of desire therefore lives.

This process, this movement, this circuit of the drive, returns no "thing" to us. Nothing, that is, but our persistent desire to *know* the site of the Other. When we get there, when we make contact with the Other, when bodies bump into other bodies, everything just vanishes. But our desire to know more simultaneously surfaces. In the circuit of the drive around identities of race, gender, activism, and nationality, which Green instigates by letting pieces of her drop for our eye to see, sites recede into nonsites, and the nonsites recede back to sites. As Smithson (1996) says, "It is always back and forth, to and fro. Discovering places for the first time, then not knowing them" (p. 195). Such is the aporic state of identity in Green's work, caught between here and there, fiction and history, self and Other. Knowing it can't be seized, it is that to which I—the critic as analysand—am *driven* to return.

REFERENCES

Barthes, R. (1977a). *Image, Music Text*, trans. S. Heath. New York: Noonday Press.
——— (1977b). *Roland Barthes by Roland Barthes*, trans. R. Howard. Berkeley: University of California Press.
——— (1978). *A Lover's Discourse, Fragments*, trans. R. Howard. New York: Hill and Wang.
——— (1981). *Camera Lucida*, trans. R. Howard, New York: Hill and Wang.
Burnham, J. (1970). Alice's head: reflections on conceptual art. *Artforum*, February, pp. 37–43.
Carson, J. (1998). (Re)Viewing Mary Kelly's *Post-Partum Document*. *Documents* 13:41–60.
Debord, G. (1994). *Society of the Spectacle*. New York: Zone.
Derrida, J. (1987). *The Postcard, From Socrates to Freud and Beyond*, trans. A. Bass. Chicago: University of Chicago Press.
Fanon, F. (1952). *Black Skin, White Masks*, trans. C. L. Markmann. London: Pluto, 1993.
Foster, H. (1996). *The Return of the Real*. Cambridge, MA: MIT Press.
Freud, S. (1899). Screen memories. *Standard Edition* 3:303–322.
——— (1920). *Beyond the Pleasure Principle*. *Standard Edition* 18:7–64.
Green, R. (1997). Partially buried. *October* 80:39–56.
Krauss, R. (1973). Sense and sensibility. *Artforum*, November, pp. 43–63.
Lacan, J. (1963–1964). Seminar XI: *The Four Fundamental Concepts of Psychoanalysis*, trans. A. Sheridan. New York: Norton, 1978.
Laplanche, J. (1976). *Life and Death in Psychoanalysis*, trans. J. Mehlman. Baltimore, MD: Johns Hopkins University Press.
Miller, J.-A. (1977–1978). Suture (elements of the logic of the signifier), trans. J. Rose. *Screen* 16:(4)24–33.
Smithson, R. (1996). *The Collected Writings*, ed. J. Flam. Berkeley: University of California Press.
Zizek, S. (1996). *The Indivisible Remainder: An Essay on Schelling and Related Matters*. New York: Verso.

Art and the Sinthome

5

Sublimation and Symptom

FRANZ KALTENBECK

Lacan invited psychoanalysts to study works of art, not as forma-
tions of the artist's unconscious but rather as the realizations of the
artist's symptom. He had learned the lessons of the theoreticians of
aesthetics like Beckett (1983) or Adorno (1973), who made it clear
that a serious creation of art is always the result of the artist's struggle
with impossibility. What we can decipher from the unconscious obeys
the laws of language that also govern the pleasure principle. But the
impossible, which is one of the Lacanian names for the Real, is "beyond the pleasure principle." Deciphering art that functions as a symptomatic support for its author requires us to forge a path beyond the
pleasure principle.[23]

The symptom in Lacan's later theory is not only a signifying formation of the unconscious through which we understand hysteric
manifestations like Dora's cough and aphonia. In his 1975–1976 semi-

---

23. This becomes clear when one reads Jean Bollack's (2001) interpretation
of the poems of Paul Celan. In contrast to many other commentaries, Bollack's work
always insists on the mortal *jouissance* of German poetry.

nar on Joyce, Lacan forged a new concept of symptom: the "sinthome." This archaic French word did not refer either to the symptom that is a sign of disease or to the symptom that results from the conflict between the subject's unconscious desire and his ego-ideal. The "sinthome," a word that includes the English noun "sin"—a very important word for Joyce—is a complex artifice that can help the artist (or any other creator) precisely to escape the mental disease that s/he incubates. That does not mean, of course, that the "sinthome" heals the subject. It can only prevent a dangerous symbolic constellation that could trigger psychosis.

"Nobody should 'apply' psychoanalysis to art." Does this mean that psychoanalysts should not interest themselves in painting, sculpture, music, literature, architecture? On the contrary. The Lacanian contempt for "applied" psychoanalysis means that the tropes of the unconscious do not *suffice* for a reading of a poetic text or a viewing of a painting. Freud himself did not stay within the boundaries of unconscious rhetoric when he wrote about *King Lear*, *The Merchant of Venice*, and Jensen's *Gradiva*, or when he interpreted the *Moses* of Michelangelo. Freud transcends the pleasure principle in his work on art and literature. (Already in "The Theme of the Three Caskets" (1913a), for example, he insists on the figure of destiny that will later become one of the representations of the death-drive and the superego.)

The approach to art through the symptom has inspired some Lacanian progressives[24] to declare Freud's theory of sublimation obsolete. The most naive idea in favor of this argument was the observation that "the artist (of our time) renounces nothing." Why only of our time? Rembrandt and Picasso had eventful sexual lives, but did they fuck when they painted? Other great composers, painters, or writers had quite an unhappy sexual life. Neither the happiness nor the unhappiness of the artist's sexuality is an argument against the theory of sublimation. The libido is not quantifiable. And Freud never

24. See, for example, Laurent (1993), who makes two claims: (1) the Freudian conception of sublimation can of course be admitted "in the symbolist and positivist horizon of the 'fin du siècle'"; (2) "nobody utilizes this word anymore" (p. 3).

presented sublimation as equivalent to sexual abstinence. On the contrary! In Lecture XXV, "Anxiety," he distinguishes clearly between abstinence and sublimation, noting that anxiety emerges if the subject cannot get rid of his libido, either by sexuality or sublimation. The confusion of sublimation with abstinence could be due to the idea attributed by Freud to Wilhelm Fliess, that the "sexual forces of the drive" of the human being accumulate during childhood (Freud 1898, p. 281). Their bursting out in puberty has to serve great cultural purposes. The principle of the accumulation of libidinal capital had been metaphorized by Freud in *The Interpretation of Dreams* (1900), where he compares the child's wish with the capitalist who can finance the project of an entrepreneur, the dream-thought. This accumulation of libido generates, according to Lacan, the object *a*, cause of desire (the "*plus-de-jouir*"). Even if Freud thought of sublimation as an antidote against anxiety he never over-estimated this process, stating clearly in Lecture XXII of his *Introductory Lectures* ("Some Thoughts on Development and Regression—Aetiology") that "sublimation is never able to deal with more than a certain fraction of libido" (Freud 1915/1917, p. 346). Sublimation simply gives another aim to the drive, another satisfaction.

For Freud sublimation was a "destiny of the drive" (*Triebschicksal*). He even wanted to write an article on sublimation for his series of metapsychological papers published between 1914 and 1917. As sublimation is a process concerning the sexual drive, it has a radical impact on the subject. The radical character of this process is emphasized by the observation that the paths of sublimation are laid down very early in the life of the child. Not everybody is capable of this "destiny of the drive." When, in *Totem and Taboo* (1913b), Freud compares the artist and the neurotic he declares that they are very close to each other; hysteria seems to him to be a "distorted" work of art. Nonetheless there is a big difference. The artist has a happier relation to the unconscious. The artist's repressions are less severe than those of the neurotic.

But in "The Ego and the Id" (1923), Freud generalizes sublimation: the concept is no longer reserved for cultural creation. Now it concerns the ego's transformation of object-libido into narcissistic libido, to which the ego gives a new aim. Freud had seen the triple problems of this generalized sublimation:

First, the transformation of object-libido into narcissistic libido begins with an abandonment of the object, and we know that such an abandonment can produce melancholia.

Second, sublimation works against Eros and so serves its opposite, the (death-) drive. Note that in his Introduction to the 1916–1917 *Lectures* sublimation meant that the sexual drive is "diverted" from its sexual aims to "higher" (nonsexual) aims. Yet Freud (1916–1917) had already felt the need to issue a warning: "But this arrangement is unstable; the sexual instincts are imperfectly tamed, and, in the case of every individual who is supposed to join in the work of civilization, there is a risk that his sexual instincts may refuse to be put to that use" (p. 23).

Third, that libidinal transformation is a "desexualization" (Freud 1923, p. 46). But if the sexual aim is abandoned, what happens to the drive? Lacan did not accept the idea of a desexualized libido. How could libido be desexualized? Was this not a contradiction? According to Lacan (1963–1964), the idea of a desexualized libido cannot make sense. What is desexualized in our life is reality.

The Freudian idea of sublimation in Lecture XXII was more optimistic. We see this in his observations about the diversion of the drive, operated by sublimation. The diversion of the drive from its original aim guarantees a greater freedom to the subject who can use this process. Drives can be diverted only if they possess enough mobility. Freud (1915–1917) reminds us that the impulses of the sexual drive "are extraordinarily plastic" (p. 345). Drives move easily from one object to another, though in the case of neurosis they get "fixed" to a certain form of satisfaction and this restricts their mobility.

The sexual drive is the raw material of culture, but culture is not possible without the repression of the drives. Here again sublimation goes its own way. The subject able to sublimate the drives is not obliged to renounce his satisfaction. So the sublimated drive does not submit either to life or to death. The innovating artist works for culture, helping to refine it, but at the same time he works against culture and civilization, trying to revolutionize them. So the innovating artist can impose himself as a subject who is part of the Other but also stays outside of the Other. His sexual drive is not the slave of sexual reproduction, and it does not work against the interests of the subject. All this is only true in the framework of the metapsychological theory of Lecture XXII that dates from 1916–1917. And even then Freud considered sublimation as a fragile destiny of drive, as we have seen. For the pessimistic Freud of 1923, sublimation was firmly in the service of the destructive drive.

In spite of all the advantages of the destiny called "sublimation," there is no reason to idealize this concept. Its triumphs are limited. It always has to struggle against anxiety, renunciation, and death, which are at work not only in the minds of individuals but also in the "discontents" of civilization. Sublimated drive has to fight against despondency. "I cannot go on; I will go on!" writes Samuel Beckett. One will never get a pure state of sublimated drive.

A SYMPTOMATIC SUBLIMATION

There is a good example of symptomatic sublimation: Freud's (1910) "Leonardo da Vinci." As an artist, Leonardo finds it increasingly difficult to finish his paintings. Freud attributes this symptom to the fact that he is both an artist and a researcher. "Great love can only come from great knowledge of the loved object," writes Leonardo in his "Treatise on Painting." In his art he sought perfection. The ideal of perfection came from his insatiable demand for knowledge. As perfection is very difficult to attain, many of his paintings were condemned to stay unfinished.

According to Freud, Leonardo had tamed his affects and transformed his passions into a "pressure to know" (Wissendrang). Unlike Goethe's Faust, he was not able to reconvert his "pressure to research" (Forscherdrang) into a "pleasure of life" (Lebenslust). Leonardo had lost not only his primary passions, love and hate, but also his ego and his ability to act in order to transform the world. His explorations of nature became endless, nonconclusive. So he lost contact with his artistic work. In following Freud, we admit that Leonardo had sublimated his sexual drive into a very powerful (*übermächtigen*) "research drive" (*Forschertrieb*). Due to the exchange of aims—research came to the place of sexual satisfaction—Leonardo's sexual life became impoverished. But why should someone convert sexuality into such a research drive?, asks Freud. And further on: How can this libidinal transformation happen in childhood? Freud's answer to these questions is not always well understood. He supposes that small children have a "desire to know" (*Wissbegierde*). They have a timeless pleasure of questioning (*Fragelust*). All their endless questions stand for a single inquiry, "Where do children come from?" So children, at least the most gifted, go through an intense "infantile sexual research" (*Infantile Sexualforschung*) that is often triggered by the birth of a little brother or sister. They never forgive their parents' false and mythological answers to their questions[25] concerning the child in the mother's womb and the role of the father. As the child's own sexual constitution is far from mature, his researches into these questions very often remain without result and are abandoned. This failure can lead to depression in the child.

The infantile sexual researches succumb to repression, together with infantile sexuality. There are now three possible outcomes: first, that the neurotic inhibition of sexual researches leads to a weakness in thinking; second, that the intellectual development is strong enough to resist repression, the subject sexualizes his thinking, and the infantile researches survive as constant ruminations; third, the rare possibility that occurred in Leonardo's case, where the libido eludes repression, is sublimated into the desire to know, and is reinforced by a powerful research drive. Here research becomes a substitute for sexual activity. As Leonardo's sexual drive was not fixed to the "original complexes of infantile sexual research," the substitution did not result in neurosis. So Leonardo succeeded in the substitution at the point where the ordinary child's desire to know is repressed. He could sublimate most of his libido into the "pressure to research." Freud (1910) considers this transformation to be "the core of his nature, and the secret of it" (p. 80). And still this sublimation is symptom-

---

25. Freud mentions the fable of the stork.

atic! Leonardo did not suffer from neurosis; he suffered from an unfulfilled sexual life. We cannot go into Freud's aetiology of Leonardo's
"ideal (sublimated) homosexuality." It is sufficient to recall Mona
Lisa's equivocal smile with "the promise of unbounded tenderness
and at the same time sinister menace" ("threat announcing disas-
ter" [*unheilverkündende Drohung*], p. 115). For ". . . like all unsatis-
fied mothers, she took her little son in place of her husband, and by
the too early maturing of his erotism robbed him of a part of his
masculinity" (p. 117).

Leonardo suffered not only from his unfulfilled sexual life but
also from an inhibition. He could not finish his later paintings, and
even his researches lack conclusion. His art and his research entered
into conflict. But what is the link between his "ideal homosexuality"
and his inhibition? Freud's idea that he left his paintings as his father
left his women is interesting, but it is not the whole explanation. In
his last chapter, Freud distinguishes between two sublimations in
Leonardo's life. The first occurred in his early childhood when he
transformed his libido into his "pressure for research." The second
sublimation takes place during his puberty. This is the moment when
he becomes an artist. But later on, the suppression of his "real sexual
life" paralyzes even his sublimated drive! He loses the power of decision; he hesitates when painting *The Last Supper*. Leonardo enters into
a very strange regression that is near to a neurotic regression. He loses
his pleasure in painting and in creating art, a pleasure he had acquired
as an adolescent. So the "second sublimation" of the sexual drive loses
its ground and he falls back on the "first sublimation"—his infantile
desire to know, preserved against repression. Leonardo becomes a
researcher, but his research is no longer in the service of his art. This
description of Leonardo's fate proves that Freud was very lucid about
the dangers of sublimation when he wrote his study on Leonardo in
1910. One could draw an analogy between the danger of sublimation
and the danger of the "sinthome": Joyce suffered a great deal when
he worked on *Finnegans Wake*!

Even if Leonardo still had in his fifties a great creative eruption—
Anna Metterza and the Gioconda—with his growing age nature became the main object of his research. Freud interprets nature as a

sublimation of his mother, whereas God—a rather impersonal god—represents Leonardo's sublimated father. In his seminar *La Relation d'Objet*, Lacan (1956–1957) elaborates on Leonardo's relation to nature. For Lacan, Leonardo does not deserve to be considered as the first scientist. He did not discover any of the laws of physics; he did not anticipate Galileo. For Leonardo nature is merely a magical, capricious being, not his Other, but rather his other. His sublimation did not produce rational research but a rather mystical and enthusiastic relation to nature as animist being.

SUBLIMATION AND THE OBJECT

In his study on Leonardo, Freud deconstructs one of the ideals of the Renaissance in showing that in his case sublimation, the very motor of his creation, was accompanied by symptom and inhibition. But sublimation is not only a "destiny of the drive." It does not raise clinical questions only. It also has an ethical dimension. Remember that for Wittgenstein, ethics and esthetics are one and the same thing. The secret of sublimation does not lie in the plasticity of the drives but in the subject's choice of a new aim for his drives. In his seminar *The Ethics of Psychoanalysis* (1959–1960), Lacan gives us a theory about the aim of sublimation. He proposes a definition of this process in which he uses the idea of "the Thing," a term to be found in Freud's "Project for a Scientific Psychology" (1895). Lacan put "the Thing" at the center of his ethics. He speaks of "the field of the Thing" (Lacan 1959–1960, p. 106), as he will speak ten years later of "a field of enjoyment." The term "field" is borrowed from physics (electric, magnetic . . . fields). Lacan claims that the Thing, and later on, enjoyment, form fields where the essential relations between the subject, his world, and his other take place. The Thing is beyond all representations, that is, beyond the domain of language. Lacan characterizes the Thing as the place of good and bad will. That means that the Thing is the place to which Kant's practical judgments refer. These judgments (of the second critique) are not limited to the "weak" morality of the good. In order to found his practical philosophy and his metaphysics of morals, Kant presupposes his *Critique of Pure Reason*. The morality of an action can only be judged on the grounds of reason and the human being must be free in order to be able to act morally. The principle of each moral action should correspond to a law that can be universally stated. (It has to be a principle valid for everyone.) This law does not depend on a "highest good" or on god. The irony of this purely formal law is—and this is what Lacan shows in "Kant avec Sade"—that it still demands an object: not a good one, but the torturing object of Sade.

Lacan insists on a distinction between the Thing and the object(s). He reads the object relation as Freud does in his (1914) paper "On Narcissism" where the object is "structured by the narcissistic relation," whereas the Thing constitutes the horizon of the drives (Lacan 1959–1960, p. 98). As long as we search only for pleasure, we turn around the Thing without approaching it. In the paper on narcissism, Freud distinguishes between idealization and sublimation. The first employs the libido of the ego; the second works with the libido of the object. Lacan's subtle reading of Freud's metapsychology brings him to a deep insight into the process of sublimation: "At the level of sublimation the object is inseparable from imaginary and especially cultural elaborations" (p. 99).[26]

Sublimation does not act on pure drive. It includes the object that is already laden with the signifiers of a given culture. But even if sublimation utilizes socially valorized objects, it implicates a transgression of the pleasure principle, as does perversion. Sublimation and perversion have two common denominators. The first is the central role of the object. In sublimation the object is "overestimated," whereas in perversion the object is the agent and the slave of the Other's *jouissance*. The second common denominator is a certain suspension of sexual *jouissance*. The true pervert seeks to satisfy the enjoyment of the Other, not his own. Of course, the Other (God) is not the victim of the torment; he is supposed to enjoy the victim's suffering. In the case of the sublimation of courtly love, The Lady is

---

26. See also pp. 113, 119, 180, where Lacan insists on the Imaginary dimension of the object. The object helps to represent the Thing that cannot be imagined.

a forbidden object. The troubadour sublimating his drive may only adore her; he could never satisfy his sexual desire with his adored Lady.

The classical Freudian symptom satisfies the drive by the substitution of one signifier for another. The girl who wants to replace her sick mother by her father's side falls sick herself. "You wanted to be your mother and now you *are*—anyhow as far as your sufferings are concerned" Freud 1921, p. 106). The girl's identification with her sick mother has created the symptom. Sublimation does not use the substitution of signifiers, it changes the aim of the drive. So what does this change of aim mean?, asks Lacan. To answer this question he coined this formula: "Sublimation raises the object to the dignity of the Thing." There is a kind of play on words ("calembour," says Lacan) in this formula: "dignité" rhymes with the German "Ding." The term "object" is equivocal. It designates mundane objects but also the object that attracts the libido. Lacan's example of Jacques Prevert's collection of matchboxes assembled along his mantelpiece is very nice. Geneviève Morel chooses Sarah Lucas' cigarette sculptures.[27] In both cases the artists' material is very ordinary stuff, and that is also true of the popular melodies that Beethoven introduced into his piano sonatas.

The strong implication of Lacan's formula lies in its desacralization of the creative process. Lacan never says that the object really comes to the place of the Thing, that it is introduced into its transcendental space! He merely points out that the object is "elevated" to the dignity of the Thing. As the Thing is not the nicest place we can think of, the words "dignity" and "to elevate" bear an ironic note. After all, sublimation is an operation with semblance.[28]

---

27. See Geneviève Morel, "Joyce's Art and Extension of the Symptom," *Manifesta 2000*, Ljubljana, July 2000.

28. "Semblance" is a notion that Lacan elaborated in his teachings following Seminar XVII, *L'envers de la psychanalyse* (1969–1970). A year after this seminar where he established his four discourses, he arrived at the conclusion that no discourse could work without semblances. The sense that emerges in the discourse of

Lacan adds a new element to the theory of this operation in his un-published seminar *La Logique du Fantasme* (1966–1967). Already in his *Ethics* seminar he had said that "in every form of sublimation emptiness is determinative" (p. 130). Now the starting point of the creative process becomes more important than its aim. Sublimation starts from an initial lack, the lack of castration (Lacan 1967, sessions of February 22, March 8). We have to distinguish this lack from the more general void created by the potter when he fabricates a vase. (See M. Heidegger's [1954] essay on the Thing to which Lacan refers in his *Ethics*.[29]) The initial lack can never be absorbed by creative work, for the creation will reproduce it. In his "Logic of Fantasy" Lacan opposes sublimation to the sexual act. He asks: "What is the structure of . . . sublimation? Unlike the simple sexual act sublimation starts from the lack and constructs its work with the help of this lack" (Lacan 1966–1967, March 8). This theory that sublimation starts from an initial lack, castration, reformulates one of the axioms of sublimation. It is a process where the most important events take place at the beginning of the artist's career, that is, in childhood.

But isn't Lacan speaking about himself when he considers the starting point of the process of sublimation? His scientific beginnings shaped many of the developments of his later work. Similarly, he looks back to his doctoral thesis on the relation between paranoia and personality, when he works on a new theory of the symptom in the mid-seventies. His seminar, *Le Sinthome* (1975–1976) is a late answer to the problems at the beginning.[30]

---

the psychoanalyst is made of semblance (*Encore*, Seminar XX (1972–1973). So semblance is—at least partially—a product of the Imaginary. In the same seminar Lacan represents it as a vector going from the Symbolic to the Imaginary. He explains of analysts that "we are not even semblance. We are, on occasion, that which can occupy that place, and allow what to reign there? Object *a*" (p. 95). Whereas the Thing is thought as being real, the object *a* participates in semblance.

29. Lacan refers to Heidegger's paper in chapter 9 of the *Ethics* seminar.

30. See on this point Geneviève Morel, "The Young Man without an Ego: A Study on James Joyce and the Mirror Stage," this volume.

THE SYMPTOM

According to Lacan, it was not Freud but Marx who introduced the symptom into modern thinking "as a sign of what does not work in the real" (Lacan, 1974–1975, session of December 10, 1974). But Marx considered only the "social symptom" (the deprivation of the proletariat by capitalism). Psychoanalysis is occupied by the "particular symptom," for example, the symptom of the obsessional for whom death is an "*acte manqué*." To formalize the relation between the symptom and the unconscious, Lacan writes the symptom as a mathematical function, $f(x)$, where "f" is the sign for function and "x" is "that element of the unconscious that can be translated by a letter." Take, for example, the name of the painter Signorelli that Freud (1901) forgot during a journey along the Dalmatian coast. This name condenses his unconscious relation to "the last things," that is, to death and sexuality. Whereas a signifier always refers to another signifier, the letter stays identical to itself, but this identity is not based on any quality. The mathematical letter—Descartes' "small letters" of algebra—is an example of the Lacanian concept of the letter. They have no sense and they are not signifiers of ordinary language. They are not defined by their opposition to other signifiers. They have no quality. But the equation constituted by such letters can refer either to a mathematical or to a physical object. There are also the letters of poetry. When a poet has chosen a word for a poetical text, it is not sufficient to replace it by its synonym to get the sense of the verse or sentence in which it occurs. In *Finnegans Wake* we can read many words that are not recognized as such, for example, "immarginable." We understand that Joyce condensed "imaginable" and "marge." But how can we know what he wanted to say when he wrote the word? To answer this question, we would have to study the relation between "image" and "marge" in Joyce's work. "Immarginable" is not a Freudian *witz*. It does not have phallic signification. To find its signification we would need to answer the following question: How does this word contribute to Joyce's relation to his *jouissance*? And to answer such a question, one sometimes needs to be very literate.

We should not confound the function of the symptom with Frege's propositional functions. Geneviève Morel has shown that propositional functions can be very useful in articulating the symptoms of psychotic patients. Propositional functions can be thought of as "sentences with holes." Let's take a very simple example. At a moment in preoedipal development, the child believes her/himself to be the unique object of its mother's desire. If nobody gives her/him a better interpretation of her/his mother's desire, s/he can maintain this belief even if s/he transfers it to other persons who have some power. We could write this belief with the help of a "sentence with a hole": "X" is the darling of—." Such a propositional function could express the symptom of X: "X is the darling of his mother," "X is the darling of his teacher," and so on. We can put many new complements at the empty place of this "sentence with the hole." The proposition with all the arguments that fit in the hole describes X's symptom. Geneviève Morel (2000) demonstrated that in some paradigmatic cases of psychosis the symptoms of the patients could be written with such propositional functions. These symptoms allowed her patients to live quite a normal life for several years. But each crisis in their lives necessitated the unconscious rewriting of these sentences with new arguments in their holes. Nevertheless the structure of the symptom's sentence stayed invariable. So the symptom gave a limited stability to these psychotics. The analyst's recognition of the symptom permits the reinforcement of this stability. Even in very serious cases of triggered psychosis, we can locate precisely the function of the symptom. So we have, for example, examined in our clinical presentations, in Lille, the case of a young man suffering from paranoia with persecution. He stated the sentence of his symptom in the following terms: "I seriously fail my oral exams." This sentence was a kind of symptomatic metaphor containing the content of his problem, the "oral." (The patient's sentence is more expressive in French. Literally, it says, "I am seriously stranded at my oral exams" (*"J'échoue largement a l'oral"*). One could read this sentence as "My drive is stranded largely at the oral zones where it is still too far from the shore." During our dialogue with the patient, we found out that the theme of orality emerged at every serious crisis of his life. (We could write "oral" in place of "f" in f (x) and the different instances of this theme in place of "x." The signifiers of orality were produced in different situations of stress and anxiety: exams, his first relation to a girl, the first questioning about sexual difference. So this patient told us that he was perfectly able to succeed in his written exams but that he fails all his oral ones. His first love was troubled. He met a girl but his parents opposed the relationship. Again, the signifier of orality played a large role. The whole theme of orality could be traced back to his childhood. In his first class at school, he had preferred a woman teacher who only worked with classes for girls. So he decided to go to her class where he was the only boy. But during this year he was so nervous and anxious that he bit his lips until they bled. Nevertheless he stayed in the class of girls, telling us that he stubbornly ("*mordicus*") maintained his decision against the authority of his mother, who wanted to send him to the class for boys. It is clear that the symptomatic function of this man has its roots in a very archaic disturbance of his sexual identity, which was already obvious when he was five years old. At each moment where this subject is threatened by the impossibility of answering a question that concerns the principles of the Symbolic (the Name-of-the-Father), he reacts by producing a signifier of the oral domain ("to bite," "to eat," "oral exams," etc.). These signifiers of his symptom are the warning signs of a great danger. In this sense his symptom is stabilized by the repetition of these signifiers. We could say that a symptom is made up of a series of "survival-reflexes" (Kacem 1997, p. 11).

Lacan was first invited by the Joycean scholar, Jacques Aubert, to the International Joyce Congress in the summer of 1975, and he continued his teaching the following academic year. Already in the Congress paper he had put the view that the biography of the Irish poet and his work were inseparable. For Lacan, Joyce's writing functioned as his symptom. The function of the symptom was close to the function of a proper name. Joyce had to create his name for himself. So his symptom became his name, "Joyce, the symptom" ("Joyce, le sinthome"). "Joyce the symptom" as "Billy the Kid." But this very particular literary work gave to its author more than a symptom and a name. It also gave him an Ego. That means that Joyce possessed neither an Ego nor a name before writing his first work.

In his seminar on the sinthome, Lacan asked the question, "Was Joyce mad?" According to Lacan, the answer is positive. Unlike many "normal" people, Joyce was aware of the strange action that language exerts on all speaking human beings. Words (*paroles*) are imposed on the speaking subject. Words are real parasites on those who speak. This imposition becomes stronger in the course of Joyce's life. He must have felt the pressure of the imposition of language. So he had to break the words down in order to dissolve their phonetic identities. In his late work, *Finnegans Wake*, he mixed English words with the words of other languages; he created new words, and abolished the identities of old ones. This is one aspect of Lacan's idea that Joyce's oeuvre had to supply the Name-of-the-father that he had rejected. Indeed his father was a very charming man, but he did not want to function as a father. This resignation is very well described by his son in the second chapter of *A Portrait of the Artist as a Young Man*. And there are also many allusions to the foreclosure of the Name-of-the-Father in *Ulysses*. For example, Stephen, the young hero of *Ulysses*, the Telemachus of the novel, searches for his father. But when Leopold Bloom offers himself as father to his young companion after their wandering through nighttown in the chapters "Circe" and "Emaeus" (episodes 15 and 16), Stephen does not accept this substitute father. Joyce's writing, his sinthome,[31] has its roots in his father even if, or perhaps because, he rejected his father through foreclosure. This is the paradox: Joyce owes many of the stories written into his work to his father, who was a brilliant storyteller. But these stories did not give his son the symbolic underpinnings that he needed as a subject. For this, Joyce had to appeal to the teachings of the Jesuits and to the Fathers of the Church, for example to St. Augustine.

---

31. Let us use the Lacanian term *sinthome* in the case of psychotics who produce works of art or at least signifying structures that protect them against the devastating effects of their madness by knotting the Real, the Symbolic, and the Imaginary, with the help of a fourth consistency, the *sinthome*, that can be a work of art.

Joyce's case is marked by serious trouble at the level of his body. In a sense he had no body. He knew it, and wrote it in *Ulysses*. His imaginary body (his body image) was not knotted into the Symbolic (language) and the Real (drive, *jouissance*). Lacan, who tried in his late seminars to adapt the theory of knots for a psychoanalytic writing of the Real, speaks of an error, a "lapsus" in the knot. The three consistencies of the Symbolic, the Imaginary, and the Real were not linked in Joyce's case. So Joyce needed a fourth dimension, a fourth consistency, his writing, his sinthome. With this consistency of the sinthome he could link the other three dimensions, and the new knot formed with four strings spared him from psychotic dissociation and decomposition.

The most intriguing aspect of the sinthome is its relation to the question of sexual difference. Joyce had a very strong and close relation to Nora Barnacle, his wife. But could he see in her a woman? Lacan doubts it. According to him, Nora fitted Joyce like a glove. The sense of this comparison is obvious: You can turn a glove—one without buttons—inside out and wear it on your other hand. So, for Lacan, Nora was the other side of "Jim," as she called him. Nora was a part of his symptom. But she was essential for him, and whenever he was tempted by another woman she would always look like Nora. "There is only one woman for Joyce, she is always the same model and he only puts on his glove with the utmost revulsion" (Lacan 1975–1976, Session 10, February 1976, p. 10).

In general, woman is the symptom of the man. Lacan's diagram of sexuation (Seminar XX, *Encore*) shows how the woman functions as the object of the man. Lacan's argument shows the lack of the sexual relation. This is in keeping with sublimation as an operation with the object that is "asexual" (*asexué*). Can the same be said of the sexual relation in the case of the psychotic? No, because in this case there is some relation between the sexes. The way in which the psychotic relates to his partner as symptom is different. The psychotic sustains *a sexual relation with the symptom*. This is clear in the case of the psychotic who wished to be a woman and was able to give up this wish when he met a hysterical woman who fell in love with him because he was a rather effeminate man. Previously, this woman had preferred homosexual men as friends and rejected virile men like her father, who could not give her enough love. The psychotic, whom she married, reminded her of her mother's tenderness. The psychotic's relation to the woman (as symptom) is determined by the relation between the sexes; it is governed by the problems of the impossible relation between men and women. The symptom is the only structure able to establish a sexual relation. *There is a sexual relation between the subject and his/her symptom. This also holds for the Joycean sinthome.*

Symptoms don't always result in creative work. They can be fatal. Such, for example, is the social symptom of fascism. People sometimes confound sadism and fascism. But it is important to say that the logic of the fantasy in the work of the Marquis de Sade is not that of fascistic ideology. Lacan, who has elaborated on Sade's logic, notes in his *Ecrits* that Sade, unlike Joyce, wanted his name to be erased from his grave. This erasure of the symbolic trace is an aspect of what Lacan calls "the second death." But remember that Sade wanted his own second death, whereas the fascists want the second death of their victims. This desire for the second death of the other manifested itself recently in the case of General Augusto Pinochet. The general thought that he and his men had a brilliant idea when they organized the disappearance without trace of the corpses of their victims. No corpse, no crime, they thought. But as Ariel Dorfman (2000) noted, Pinochet, in organizing the disappearance of these corpses "captured himself deliciously in the nets of his own perversity." In fact the Supreme Court of Chile stated that the disappearance of the corpses organized by the Chilean general constituted the crime of kidnapping. Such a crime comes to an end only when the bodies of the victims reappear. So the Supreme Court, considering Pinochet a mass kidnapper, suppressed his Parliamentary immunity. Pinochet organized the disappearance of the bodies of thousands of innocents, but was trapped by this very act against the symbolic existence of his victims. In reality he acted according to the will of the fascist symptom. Following the Nazis, the fascists try to destroy the symbolic coordinates of the subjects. They deny their human rights if they are of another race, and sometimes they kill them twice: first physically, then symbolically, abolishing their names, their existences, their graves. Neither the Nazis nor fascists like Pinochet succeed in erasing the symbolic traces of the people they killed. In the case of Pinochet, the strategy of the second death of the victims now produces the proof of his culpability.

Art and creation are the very opposite of the abolition of the symbolic trace of the subject. We have no portrait of Sade but we have his writings. In the case of Joyce, in danger of losing his bodily consistency, his writing/symptom gave him a name, a body, and an Ego. But what is at stake in a work of art if it is not the answer to a great danger?

* * *

Sublimation and symptom are both indispensable concepts of psychoanalysis. One cannot substitute the Lacanian "sinthome" for sublimation. But it would be equally wrong to think that sublimation is a normal process and sinthome only a pathological structure. Freud's work on Leonardo shows that sublimation does not always avoid symptom or inhibition. Both sublimation and sinthome go beyond the pleasure principle. But it is also true that sublimation tackles the Real with the help of semblance, whereas the sinthome already takes part in the Real. The sinthome invented by Lacan proves the urgency of art.

REFERENCES

Adorno, W. (1973). *Asthetische Theorie*. Frankfurt: Suhrkamp.
Beckett, S. (1983). La peinture de Van Velde ou le monde et le pantalon; peintres de l'empechement. In *Disjecta*, ed. R. Cohn, pp. 118–137. London: John Calder.
Bollack, J. (2001). *Poésie Contre Poésie. Celan et la Litterature*. Paris: PUF.
Dorfman, A. (2000). *Le Monde*, August 11.
Freud, S. (1895). Project for a scientific psychology. *Standard Edition* 1:295–397.
———— (1898). Sexuality in the aetiology of the neuroses. *Standard Edition* 3: 263–285.

————— (1900). *The Interpretation of Dreams. Standard Edition* 4/5:xxiii–627.

————— (1901). The psychopathology of everyday life. *Standard Edition* 6.

————— (1910). *Leonardo da Vinci and a Memory of his Childhood. Standard Edition* 11:63–137.

————— (1913a). The theme of the three caskets. *Standard Edition* 12:289–301.

————— (1913b). *Totem and Taboo. Standard Edition* 13:1–161.

————— (1914). On narcissism. *Standard Edition* 14:73–102.

————— (1915–1917). *Introductory Lectures on Psychoanalysis. Standard Edition* 15/16.

————— (1921). Group psychology and the analysis of the ego. *Standard Edition* 18:69–143.

————— (1923). *The Ego and the Id. Standard Edition* 19:12–66.

Heidegger, M. (1954). Das Ding. In *Vortr ge und Aufs tze*, pp. 157–175. Pfullingen: Verlag Günter Neske, 1978.

Kacem, M. B. (1997). *L'Anteforme.* Auch: Editions Tristam.

Lacan, J. (1956–1957). Seminar IV: *La Relation d'Objet.* Paris: Seuil, 1994.

————— (1959–1960). Seminar VII: *The Ethics of Psychoanalysis.* London: Routledge, 1992.

————— (1963–1964). Seminar XI: *The Four Fundamental Concepts of Psychoanalysis.* London: Hogarth and the Institute of Psychoanalysis, 1974.

————— (1966–1967). Seminar XIV: *La logique du fantasme.* Unpublished.

————— (1969–1970). Seminar XVII: *L'envers de la psychanalyse.* Paris: Seuil, 1991.

————— (1972–1973). Seminar XX: *Encore,* ed. J.-A. Miller. Paris: Seuil, 1975.

————— (1974–1975). Seminar XXII: *R.S.I.* Ornicar? *Periodique du Champ freudien,* nos. 2–5. Paris: Navarin.

————— (1975–1976). Seminar XXIII: *Le Sinthome.* Ornicar? *Periodique du Champ freudien,* nos. 6–11. Paris: Navarin.

Laurent, W. E. (1993). Styles de vie. *La Cause freudienne: Revue de psychanalyse* 25:3–4.

Morel, G. (2000). *Joyce's art and extension of the symptom.* Paper given at *Manifesta,* Ljubljana.

6

A Young Man without an Ego: A Study on James Joyce and the Mirror Stage[32]

GENEVIÈVE MOREL

By presenting the art of James Joyce as a *sinthome* in his seminar of 1975, Lacan introduced a conceptual innovation into psychoanalysis. "*Sinthome*" is an old French spelling of "symptom" dating from 1495. Rabelais, who was a doctor, wrote it in this way. In French the two words are pronounced differently. Until this seminar of Lacan's, psychoanalysts (including Lacan himself) had approached art with the Freudian concept of sublimation (*Sublimierung*).[33] However, when he was invited to a symposium on Joyce, Lacan, who had been elaborating a new theory of the symptom since 1974, broke with psychoanalytic classicism by leaving sublimation behind and invented the concept of the *sinthome* for Joyce. He thus designates a transforma-

---

32. This text derives from a seminar entitled "*Les identifications et le symptôme*" delivered at the *Clinical Section* of Lille in 1997–1998. I would like to thank Annie Bourgois and Sylvie Nève for their help in establishing this text. (Trans. note: Throughout the text *ego* is in English in the original.)

33. The difference between these two concepts will not be the subject of our study here. The reader is referred to the article by Franz Kaltenbeck in this volume.

tion of the initial symptom of the subject by the *savoir-faire* of the artist. Before elaborating this point, it might be useful to briefly situate Lacan's conception of the symptom when he undertook to work on Joyce.[34]

FROM METAPHOR TO THE BORROMEAN KNOT

The most classic Lacanian theory is that of the symptom as a metaphor, that is to say as a substitution of one term (the signifier of the symptom) for another (the repressed signifier) (Lacan 1966). This is what a conversion symptom is, for example the aphonia of Dora, the young woman in analysis with Freud. The symptom is lifted when the word associated with the symptom appears in the treatment, *unvermögend*, namely the repressed signifier of the father's impotence that equivocates on his fortune and wealth. The aphonia in fact mimes the sexual relations of her father, impotent and wealthy, with whom Dora identifies, in an oral relation with his mistress, Frau K. Such a conception of the symptom makes it a type of unconscious formation that can disappear: it suffices to produce the repressed signifier to unmake the metaphor and unknot the symptom. As a metaphor, the symptom contains within itself the possibility of its own cure.

In the seminar *R.S.I.* (1974–1975), the definitions of the symptom entail entirely different consequences. For example, with the definition of the symptom as "that which doesn't work out in the real," Dora's symptom can no longer be limited to its conversions. Indeed, Dora gives multiple signs of what does not work out in the real for her. In *L'envers de la psychanalyse*, Lacan includes here everything that divides the subject, and turns it into a multiform "hysterical complex" that is unresolved by the enunciation of the *unvermögend* alone, as one sees in the Freudian observation. A second definition of the symptom in *R.S.I:* "the symptom can only be defined as the way in which each subject enjoys [*jouit*] the unconscious, insofar as the unconscious determines him," shows us its double link with *jouissance* and the

---

34. Cf. also Morel 2000, chs. 2 and 4.

unconscious. *Jouissance* is here to be taken as the excess in relation to the Freudian pleasure principle, which is a principle of homeostasis: an excess of pleasure or suffering. In this sense, what Freud called "the strange satisfaction" of the drive in the symptom can be renamed as *jouissance* and characterized as real, and even as "that which does not work out in the real." The determination of the symptom always comes from the unconscious, in other words from the symbolic,[35] but this fixes something of *jouissance*: in this way the symptom becomes a function of *jouissance*. Psychoanalysis touches upon the symptom insofar as it is homogeneous with it, operating from the symbolic (speech) toward the real (*jouissance*) by means of interpretation. The equivocation of interpretation responds to the equivocation of the symptom in which *jouissance* remains a prisoner, aiming at it to produce effects of sense. However, to operate on, or to relieve, is not to remove, and if, at the end of an analysis, the symptom is no longer touched by interpretation, it remains no less present, and becomes from then on the irremovable and real framework (*monture*) of the subject. The symptom becomes transformable, but not curable.

In *R.S.I.* and in the following year in his seminar on Joyce, Lacan envisages a new function of the symptom, which would be to supplement the Name-of-the-Father. His initial theory was that the presence of the Name-of-the-Father in neurosis and perversion allowed the subject to avoid the madness that its absence (foreclosure) unleashes in psychosis. If Lacan does not renounce his characterization of psychosis as the foreclosure of the Name-of-the-Father, he does not make it strictly equivalent to madness either, and thus takes account of the variety of clinical forms of psychosis and its compatibility with "normality." In certain cases of psychoses, a symptom makes things hold together and supplements the foreclosure of the Name-of-the-Father: Lacan will call this the *sinthome*. This type of symptom would also assume another function of the Name-of-the-Father, nomination. The symptom thus inscribes itself in the Lacanian theory of the Borromean knot.

---

35. As "the unconscious is structured like a language" (Lacan). The unconscious, speech, and language are of the symbolic register.

The most simple Borromean knot consists of three rings that one can materialize with pieces of string. The three rings are not knotted two by two, but by three, so that if any one of the three rings is cut the knot becomes untied and each ring is freed (Figure 6-1).

The three rings correspond respectively to the three registers: the real (*jouissance*, the letter, writing), the symbolic (speech, language, the unconscious), and the imaginary (images, meaning). Certain subjects "function" like borromean knots, but for others the three rings will be badly knotted through a fault at the start, and a fourth ring, that of the *sinthome*, would be necessary to ensure that the knot holds. This fourth ring, the *sinthome*, functions analogously to that of the Name-of-the-Father: "the father is in sum nothing but a symptom or a *sinthome*." Lacan develops his theory of the symptom on the basis of the case of Joyce.

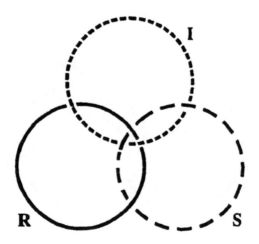

R = Real   S = Symbolic   I = Imaginary

R > S > I > R   > = passes over

Figure 6–1: The Borromean knot with three rings

JOYCE'S KNOT BEFORE THE SINTHOME

Lacan's hypothesis is that of an error from the start, of a primary fault in Joyce's knot, which through this fact is not Borromean: the rings of the symbolic and the real have been knotted directly to each other. R (the real) and S (the symbolic) are knotted together (Figure 6–2), which is not the case in a Borromean knot in which, let us remember, to cut one ring is to release all three (thus, two rings have never been knotted to each other). The imaginary (I) is, in the case of Joyce, simply wedged between R and S; thus it can slide between the two since it is not secured by anything (Figure 6–3). According to Lacan, "the epiphanies are always linked to the real, a fantastic thing—Joyce himself does not speak of them otherwise. It is quite clear that the epiphany is that which, thanks to the fault, makes the unconscious and the real knot themselves" (Session of May 11, 1976, p. 9). Thus the epiphanies are situated at the points where the real and the symbolic link themselves together on the knot.

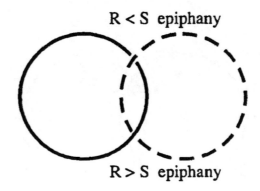

R < S epiphany

R > S epiphany

R and S are knotted together

> passes over   < passes under

Figure 6–2: The fault in Joyce's knot

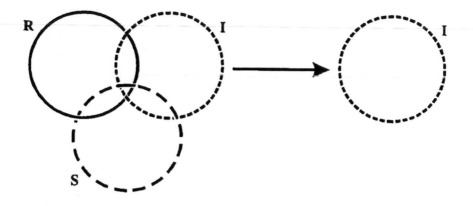

The fault knots R and S together. I slides between the two.

$$R < I < S$$

Figure 6–3: Joyce's knot before the sinthome

THE EPIPHANY

The term "epiphany" was used by Joyce as a concept intended to describe an aesthetic literary experience. He gives it a definition in *Stephen Hero* (1966): "By an epiphany he meant a sudden spiritual manifestation, whether in the vulgarity of speech or of gesture or in a memorable phase of the mind itself" (p. 215). Joyce speaks of it again as "trivial incidents." He refers himself to one of Dante's works, *The Eloquence of Vulgar Language*. He also notes: "He believed that it was for the man of letters to record these epiphanies with extreme care, seeing that they themselves are the most delicate and evanescent moments."

Joyce wrote his epiphanies between 1903 and 1904. In 1904, he wrote *Stephen Hero*—which would not be published until 1914—and the *Portrait of the Artist*, which was to be refused by the editor, leading him to write *A Portrait of the Artist as a Young Man*, which is the text commented on by Lacan in his seminar *Le Sinthome*. In *A Por-*

trait of the Artist as a Young Man (1916) and in *Ulysses* (1922), Joyce disseminates certain epiphanies. But in *Ulysses*, as Jacques Aubert reminds us, he condemns the epiphanies with irony: "Remember your epiphanies written on green oval leaves, deeply deep, copies to be sent if you died to all the great libraries of the world, including Alexandria" (Joyce 1922, p. 34).

Joyce associated the epiphanies with the beautiful and with *claritas*, one of the three qualities of the beautiful according to St. Thomas Aquinas. The others are wholeness (*integras*) and harmony (*consonantia*). *Claritas* translates itself as brightness, luminosity, radiance. Aubert (1982) signals the reference to Plotinus: a "light upon the symmetry of things" (p. liv). Beauty is in the revelation of meaning and truth. Joyce evokes "the gropings of a spiritual eye" (Aubert notes the equivocation in English between I and Eye), which seeks to grasp a precise focus for the object of epiphany: "The moment the focus is reached the object is epiphanized," says Joyce in *Stephen Hero*. *Claritas* has a relation with *quidditas* (quiddity: the whatness of the thing). In the *Portrait*,[36] Joyce gives the following explications.

1. *integras* corresponds to grasping the object as *an* integral thing.

2. *consonantia* corresponds to the recognition of the structure of the object, in its organization, and the object as a *thing*.

3. *claritas* signifies that this object is *the* object: "that thing that it is and no other thing" (Joyce 1916, p. 217). "Its soul its whatness, leaps to us from the vestment of its appearance. The soul of the commonest object, the structure of which is so adjusted, seems to us radiant. The object achieves its epiphany" (Joyce 1966, pp. 217–218).

In the *Portrait*, Stephen (the hero) further defines what *claritas* is. He first rejects the idea according to which it would be the presence of God or of the idea (in the Platonic sense) in the thing. The radiance of which he speaks is the scholastic *quidditas*, the *whatness*

---

36. Trans. note: The passage in question, drawn from chapter V of *A Portrait of the Artist as a Young Man*, is, in fact, a rewriting of the discussion of Aquinas and the epiphany in *Stephen Hero*.

of a thing. This supreme quality is felt by the artist when the asthetic image is first conceived in his imagination. The mind in that mysterious instant Shelley likened beautifully to a fading coal. Other formulations of Joyce are: "an enchantment of the heart" and "the luminous silent stasis" (Joyce 1916, p. 217). Aubert has a thesis on the epiphanies of Joyce. He brings it close to the Platonic attempt to grasp "the splendor of truth," namely a fantasmatic evocation (I-Eye). Here "spiritual" is to be taken in the sense of fantasy. In such a reading, the epiphany would describe an imaginary scenario in which the desire of the subject would be presented in a disguised form. It would not concern a representation, but rather a repetition in which the subject would be trying to "formulate himself in relation to a series of objects which would be as many masks, vacillating between language and silence, in the gaps of the signifier" (Aubert 1982, p. 217). Furthermore, he notes that "the alienation of the subject in his objects remains essentially misrecognized." Thus, it seems, if we have followed accurately, that Aubert reads the epiphanies according to the Lacanian formula of the obsessional fantasy, which establishes a relation between a subject, for whom the scopic drive is prevalent (I-Eye), and a series of objects or counterparts.

However, doesn't the epiphany rather bear witness to the moment at which speech has been heard by the poet, and at which he transmits it? It is as if Joyce wanted to write a voice. If we read "Vilanelle of the Temptress," which introduces the definition of the epiphany in *Stephen Hero*, we see that what it concerns is a dialogue between a man and a woman, with blanks, silences, points of suspension. In *R.S.I.*, Lacan makes an analogy between the symptom and points of suspension in writing, which are the sign that it does not stop: for the symptom "does not stop writing itself" for the subject. The epiphany transforms a received speech, with its blanks and aporias, into a writing riddled with points of suspension. The dialogue of the "Vilanelle" is enigmatic, constituted of allusive enunciations. Lacan situates enigma "in the relation between the enunciation and the statement," more precisely as the passage of the enunciation into the statement "The enunciation is an enigma." It thus characterizes the epiphany: "Which is why an enigma brought to the power of writing is worth stopping on." The relation of the enunciation to the enigma, evident in the statement, can only transmit itself through this special form of writing. In the epiphany, speech (S) passes into writing (R) without the restitution of meaning (I), requiring an explication of the incomplete statement, its circumstances and contexts. Here is the knotting of the symbolic and the real in a way that does not implicate the imaginary (Figure 6–3). We are thus putting the accent on this passage (of the symbolic into the real) and upon this transmission, rather than on fantasy.

Another reading of the "Vilanelle" passage could point to the foreclosure of the phallic signification[37] that "normally" attempts to reduce the enigma of the sexual relation. Here the enigma remains gaping. This first epiphany takes place against the background of Stephen's mother's insistence on religion and a dispute with her son on this subject. Stephen reflects on the attachment of women to God. They love god more than men (they: his mother and his sweetheart, Emma). The "Vilanelle" passage evokes the enigma of the woman and her relation to the father, to God, and this is rendered infinite through the absence of all phallic signification.

In the *Epiphanies*, *Ulysses*, and *Finnegans Wake*, we encounter again and again a suspended, nonexplicit, and allusive aspect of writing. In this sense, *Ulysses* and *Finnegans Wake* prolong the epiphany, and render it finally superfluous by generalizing it. All writing "epiphanizes itself"—and this goes hand in hand with the disappearance of the epiphany as a literary object in itself. It is overtaken, for it is disseminated everywhere. In this sense, there is a history to Joyce's writing that we can read as a transformation of an initial symptom—this fault in the knotting of the real and the symbolic materialized by the epiphany when Joyce is still a young writer—into a *sinthome*. The

---

37. We are referring here to the Lacanian theory of the paternal metaphor, a rewriting of the Oedipus complex. In neurosis, the Name-of-the-Father is accompanied by the phallic signification that occupies the sexual field. In psychosis, the foreclosure of the phallic signification is a consequence of the foreclosure of the Name-of-the-Father. Cf. *A question preliminary to any possible treatment of psychosis*, in Lacan 1966, p. 200.

sinthome is not contemporary with the epiphany as such, but rather consists in a progressive construction, in the putting into place of something that did not exist from the start. The initial symptom, the initial kernel of Joyce's *sinthome*, is perceptible also in his precocious relation to speech, as a child. Lacan affirms that "something in the order of speech is imposed upon him" (Session of February 17, 1976). At the beginning of chapter 2 of *A Portrait of the Artist as a Young Man*, Joyce comments upon the way in which he listened to the dialogues between his father and his uncle Charles: "Words which he did not understand he said over and over to himself until he had learned them by heart: and through them he had glimpses of the real world about him" (p. 164). Even then, when still a very young child, Joyce thought of seizing the real directly by means of a signifier outside-sense, conveyed among others by the voice of his father. Later, he will think of transmitting this signifier outside-sense (S) (the enunciation of the epiphany), in writing (R). In both cases, sense is not absent, but is put aside, between parentheses.

Let's stress the relative absence of the imaginary in the epiphany. The attempt to grasp the beautiful is linked to the intersection between the real and the symbolic, not to the attempt to grasp meaning that would imply the imaginary. It is an ineffable intuition, but one that can be written. *Claritas* comes "from a leap," not through an explication. One can note the difference of this to the memoirs of President Schreber. Schreber "does not write," but tells us through writing, he addresses a message to us. He recounts what happens to him, he testifies to it. By contrast, Joyce transmits an experience to us without aiming at what we might make of it. He does not say, as Schreber does, "all non-sense annuls itself." He attempts rather to inscribe the nonsensical part of the real in writing. Hence, the readers of Joyce (the researchers) who track meaning, meanings—it is what he wanted.

THE SLIPPING OF THE IMAGINARY

Lacan's hypothesis is that the imaginary did not hold for Joyce (cf. Figure 6–3). The key moment when the imaginary constitutes itself, "the mirror stage" (Lacan 1966, pp. 1–7), between 6 and 18 months, is the child's recognition of the image of its body in the mirror. This recognition is rendered possible through the mediation of the adult (the mother or a substitute) who, having made the child the object of her gaze and of her desire, establishes a relation of belonging between the child and its own image and founds the narcissism of the subject. This moment is the cause of a fundamental alienation for the subject in the world of images. Indeed, the *ego*, constituted by the identification with the image of the body in the mirror, appears in a position of mastery at a moment of great feebleness and dependence at which the child cannot walk or speak. This image of mastery is the proto-type of the strong ego of the neurotic, and also of his imaginary rivalry with counterparts who will appear to him all his life with the deceitful, imposing bearing that derives from this original imaginary matrix. The counterparts, others, objects of desire, are taken in this alienating dialectic of transitivism that one can observe openly in the young child: the object is desirable only if it belongs to another, the difference between oneself and the other remains indistinct. From this moment, the body of the subject appears to him as an image, and all the more so because he apprehends his interiority very badly as well as the functioning of the drive. This image founds the "him or me" aspect of paranoia that can open onto murder or suicide, or give the subject the intimate sentiment of being dead. In schizophrenia, the failure of the mirror stage can go as far as the nonrecognition of the image of the body in the mirror and the consequences of the often delusional relation of the subject with his own body. Thus, the subject's relation to the imaginary is indexed upon his relation to his own body, which is above all a relation to its image. Hence, the attention with which Lacan examined this point in relation to Joyce.

He supports his argument with a passage from the *Portrait*.

There is a confidence which Joyce extends to us. For some reason connected with Tennyson, Byron, poets, his comrades tie him to a barbed wire fence, and one named Heron—a name which is not indifferent—who directs the whole affair, and beat him for some time. Joyce wonders why, now that the thing is over, he does not

bear a grudge. Thereby, metaphorising his relation to his own body,
he notes that the whole affair has emptied itself of its contents,
like the peel of a fruit. [Lacan, Session of May 11, 1976, p. 6)

In fact, it concerns a complex passage, which we can cut into three
scenes. The scene evoked by Lacan is the second scene, which brings
back a childhood memory. It is preceded by a first scene, from adolescence, and is followed by a third at the theater where the hero is
preparing to go on stage. The scene commented on by Lacan is thus
a "scene within a scene." It is evoked in the course of an account that
is contemporaneous with the first and third scene that it interrupts
as a reminiscence. This stylistic procedure recalls the "play within a
play" of *Hamlet* (Act III, scene ii), which is the most real scene represented in the play, the fiction of the fiction, or the dream within a
dream signaled by Freud as the passage to what is most real in the
dream.[38]

THE FIRST SCENE

In 1898 Joyce is 16 years old, a key year of his adolescence, his last
year in college. It is a moment that precedes the renunciation of his
intention to take his vows. The other important person in the scene
is Heron whose name also happens to be that of a bird with a big beak,
which, furthermore, is homophonic to "Hero" (cf. *Stephen Hero*): He
is often surprised that Heron has a bird-like head, while carrying the
name of a bird. Heron is his double and his rival: "the rivals were
school friends. They sat together in class, knelt together in the chapel,

---

38. What is dreamt in a dream after waking from the "dream within a dream"
is what the dream-wish seeks to put in the place of an obliterated reality. "It is safe
to suppose, therefore, that what has been 'dreamt' in the dream is a representation
of the reality, the true recollection, while the continuation of the dream, on the
contrary, merely represents what the dreamer wishes . . . if a particular event is
inserted into a dream as a dream by the dream-work itself, this implies the most
decided confirmation of the reality of the event—the strongest *affirmation* of it"
(Freud 1900, p. 338).

talked together after beads over their lunches."[39] They are the two
best students. Heron has even got a sort of beak, a cane. He is accompanied by a dandyish boy, Wallis, sporting a cigarette-holder. After
having dared him to imitate the rector on stage (an allusion to the
third scene), Heron provokes Joyce-Stephen in relation to his father,
then with regard to a young girl who was interested in Stephen and is
due to attend the evening's theatrical representation. Heron mocks
him with regard to the girl and hits him lightly on the calf with his
cane. Stephen does not feel any anger, but the sentiment of having
had enough: "his face mirrored his rival's false smile." "Admit," said
Heron, striking him again. And Stephen, ironically, recites the *confiteor*,
with "irreverence." It is in this way that he finds that "a sudden memory
had carried him to another scene called up, as if by magic, at the
moment he had noted the faint cruel dimples at the corners of Heron's
smiling lips and had felt the familiar stroke of the cane against his
calf and had heard the familiar word of admonition: 'Admit.'" The
voice saying "Admit" and the "familiar" striking of the cane are traits
of repetition that make the childhood scene (which had taken place
five years previously) emerge, and that we here designate as the second scene.

THE SECOND SCENE

The second scene takes place in 1893, at Belvedere College. Stephen
is 11 years old, and has just entered his first year in a school run by
Jesuits. The scene begins with a metaphor concerning the blows of
life: "His sensitive nature was still smarting under the lashes of an
undivined and squalid way of life." Stephen begins to write. One day
the teacher declares, "This fellow has heresy in his essay." Stephen is
"unmasked" as a heretic and an unbeliever (which prefigures his future struggle with religion). He submits to the teacher by cleverly
correcting the incriminating formulation. When the class is over

---

39. *Portrait,* op. cit., p. 78.

Heron confronts him, already carrying his cane. He is accompanied by the dunce Boland and the idler Nash. It is then that the dispute over writers that Lacan alludes to takes place. Stephen defends Newman and Byron; Heron, Tennyson. The trio make fun of him; Stephen holds firm and insults Boland. Heron calls Byron a heretic, then bursts out, "Here, catch hold of this heretic." Stephen is thus beaten with lashes of the cane, then shoved up against the barbed wire of an enclosure, his clothes are torn (the barbed wire echoing with the beak of the heron). Stephen refuses to answer to Heron's command, "Admit" (the heresy of Byron). So unfolds the second scene, which is remembered while he recites the *confiteor* of the first scene. Let's go back to the first scene.

A RETURN TO THE FIRST SCENE: RAGE

Stephen thus asks himself why he does not become angry with them, since

> He had not forgotten a whit of their cowardice and cruelty but the memory of it called forth no anger from him. All the descriptions of the fierce love and hatred which he had met in books had seemed to him therefore unreal. Even that night as he stumbled homewards along Jones's Road he had felt that some power was divesting him of that sudden woven anger as easily as a fruit is divested of its soft ripe peel. [Joyce 1916, p. 84]

The metaphor makes anger into a tissue, a clothing; the anger is like the skin of a fruit that falls away when peeled. The scene links immediately with the third scene.

THE THIRD SCENE

Stephen listens to the applause of the spectacle that has just begun. He thinks of the young girl and of her shawl, which is the only thing about her that he remembers (again, a piece of clothing, an envelope of the body). Then he is called and he thinks of his father: "In the profane world, as he foresaw, a worldly voice would bid him raise up his father's fallen state by his labors"; further on: "he thought he saw a likeness between his father's mind and that of this smiling well-dressed priest."

The three scenes follow one another in the narration. They correspond to three ages. The first scene, comic, is from adolescence.[40] The second scene, tragic and real, with the slipping of the imaginary, is from childhood. The third scene, with his entrance on stage at the theater, concerns the question of the woman, of the *semblants* between the sexes, and of the father, who introduces the young man to maturity. In fact, one even sees "his forehead . . . being wrinkled" as he is made up by "the elderly man."

Let's focus on the slipping of the image of the body in scene 2. The scene evokes the mirror stages in many ways:

1. Heron is Stephen's double, and this even at the level of the name, for both have bird names: Stephen names himself Dedalus, in other words the "hawklike man" (1916, pp. 173–174).

2. The aggressivity characteristic of the identificatory tension between the ego and its mirror image is apparent in that the two boys are qualified as "rivals" and in the presence of Heron's beak.

3. The problematic of recognition is readable through the reference to the master in the three scenes (he who calls him a heretic in the second scene, he whom he is asked to caricature in the first scene).

4. Transitivism: the object of desire and of rivalry is represented by the young girl.

5. The gaze made present in the beak of Heron; the evocation of eyes torn out by eagles (birds again) in the first chapter (p. 8) resonates with the barbed wire of the second scene: "he torn flushed and panting, stumbled after them half blinded with tears, clenching his fists madly and sobbing." We were introduced to the problematic of the mirror stage, through the reference to the mother's mirror, in which Stephen contemplates himself for a long time before the three

---

40. Scene 1, adolescence: In thinking of the girl, "he seemed to be clothed in the real apparel of boyhood." At the end of the chapter, after the failed meeting with the young girl, Stephen goes to see a prostitute.

scenes unfold (p. 73). Many passages from the *Portrait* evoke the same mechanism of the shedding of the image of the body, figured as a skin or an item of clothing. This shedding is accompanied by a disappearance of the anticipated affect of anger, and sometimes of a rising of disgust with himself. Here are a few examples : "A power, akin to that which had often made anger or resentment fall from him, brought his steps to rest" (p. 89) or even, "A brief anger had often invested him but he had never been able to make it an abiding passion and had always felt himself passing out of it as if his very body were being divested with ease of some outer skin or peel" (p. 152). This relation between the shedding of the body and anger is repetitive. According to Lacan, what slips away from Joyce in these moments is "the confused image that [he has] of [his own] body" and not his unconscious.[41] It concerns the detaching—presented as an act of the subject—of the image of the body as a skin, "like someone who brackets off and drives out bad memories" (and it is precisely in a textual parenthesis, the second scene, that the memory returns). Lacan adds: "This manner of letting the relation to the body drop is highly suspect for an analyst." The term "letting drop" (*liegen lassen*: to let everything drop) is borrowed from Schreber, who uses it to qualify his relation to God. This latter is traced to the relation with his mother, rendered prevalent through the foreclosure of the Name-of-the-Father. In Joyce's case it concerns letting the image of the body drop, as a pathology of the mirror stage.[42] Once the question of the relation of the subject to his *ego* is posed, to his *ego* as Lacan calls it here: if Joyce's *ego* is not supported by the image of the body (through the slipping of the imaginary) how does it function? Does he have one,

---

41. The rejection or the slipping of the unconscious is more characteristic of mania.

42. It is interesting to observe that the three clinical cases of psychoses commented on by Lacan, Aimée, Schreber, and Joyce, are centered on the mirror stage, though of course in different ways. The problematic of the *ego* takes up the mirror stage once again, in terms of the Borromean knot. One can mark three dates for the Lacanian elaboration of the mirror stage: 1936 (the original text); 1966: *Écrits*, "De nos antécédents" (Paris: Seuil), p. 68 sq.; and 1976 in the seminar on Joyce, *Le Sinthome*.

and if so what is it made of? Before attempting to respond to these questions, let us look into the question of Joyce's psychosis, and the problem of nomination.

"NAMES"

Let's read what follows from the three scenes from the end of chapter 2 that we have just commented on and that are taken up by Aubert (1982) in his introduction to the complete works of Joyce in the edition of the *Pléiade* library. Lacan might have found here a confirmation of his idea that the function of the father is not reduced to that of being a name (Name-of-the-Father), but that the father must also assume the function of nomination. This idea is in fact found in *R.S.I.*: "I reveal the radical function of the Name-of-the-Father, which is to give things a name, with all the consequences which this brings, right up to the question of *jouissance*."

Stephen's father has brought him to Cork where he comes to attend the auction of his father's mortgaged property. Richard Ellmann (1959) tells us in his biography of Joyce that the first mortgage of his father's properties occurred at the time that May was pregnant with James, and associates the paternity of John Joyce with the mortgage in a significant way.[43] During the trip, Stephen experiences a feeling of dispossession. His father takes him to the university where he studied. He wanted to rediscover his initials etched on the wooden benches of the anatomy lecture theater. His initials are the same as those of his son (in reality J. J., in the novel S. D.). While they are there, the word "foetus," cut into the desk, jumps to his son's eyes. In this instant, Stephen experiences a curious moment: "It shocked to find in the outer world a trace of what he had deemed till then a brutish and individual malady of his own mind." The fact of finding the initials of his father—his own—on the wood does not stop anything: he is

---

43. "John Joyce applied himself with equal diligence to the begetting of children and the contracting of mortgages on his inherited properties . . . John Joyce filled his house with children and with debts" (Ellmann 1959, pp. 19–20).

"always weak and humble towards others, restless and sickened of himself," and further on, "The letters cut in the stained wood of the desk stared upon him, mocking his bodily weakness and futile enthusiasms and making him loathe himself for his own mad and filthy orgies." Later, he experiences the impression of being effaced—like an image: "He had not died but he had faded out like a film in the sun. He had been lost or had wandered out of existence for he no longer existed," and "By his monstrous way of life he seemed to have put himself beyond the limits of reality" (Joyce 1916, pp. 92–97).

At this moment, "He could respond to no earthly or human appeal," and is left "wearied and dejected by his father's voice." He attempts to pull himself together by saying, "I am Stephen Dedalus. I am walking beside my father whose name is Simon Dedalus. We are in Cork, in Ireland. Cork is a city. Our room is in the Victoria Hotel. Victoria and Stephen and Simon. Simon and Stephen and Victoria. Names." "The memory of his childhood suddenly grew dim. ... He recalled only names: Dante, Parnell, Clane, Clongowes."

This sequence can be read as a moment at which he had to support the function of nomination himself because of the foreclosure of the Name-of-the-Father. The preceding page of the novel concerns the relation between father and son in Joyce's family over two generations. Stephen's father says: "I'm talking to you as a friend, Stephen. I don't believe in playing the stern father. I don't believe a son should be afraid of his father. No, I treat you as your grandfather treated me when I was a young chap. We were more like brothers than father and son." The father prolongs with his own son his own father's renunciation of his paternal role. What is in question is a diminution of the symbolic transmission of paternity from father to son. They are on the same level, like counterparts, like brothers.

Let us resume our interpretation of this sequence:

1. First, the relations between the father and the son: How can we define them? By a *Verwerfung* (rejection): the renunciation of paternity.

2. The foreclosure of the Name-of-the-Father is materialized in the narrative through the absence of the father's name on the college bench: "he's not his father's son," (p. 97) said an old man.

3. The foreclosure of phallic signification, associated with the Name-of-the-Father, brings to light, amid the graffiti on the desk, a word that interpellates the subject, engraved: "fetus," namely the being of the subject in a nonsymbolic form (he is not the son of his father but a misbirth).

4. An extreme affliction follows that translates as the effacement of himself as identified with an image, which occurs through the evocation of fading memories, the memory of a dream of his own death in childhood that we can situate as the sentiment of being dead as a subject in the past.

5. "Names": An act of nomination that permits him to represent himself as a subject, to keep going. He calls on the names of his childhood that are prestigious names like Dante, the name of his wet nurse, or Parnell. Such is the nomination that he himself constructs in order to supplement the bankruptcy of paternity. Nomination is crucial in Joyce's work, as Aubert (2000) has shown by studying the disappearance of the pseudonym Stephen Dedalus, which gave way to the advent of his own name, in 1907, at the time of the birth of his daughter Lucia, the writing of the story "The Dead" of *Dubliners*, and before rewriting the *Portrait* (p. 55). Joyce supported his own name thanks to his *oeuvre* of writing—"rooted in his father," says Lacan (one can see it in *Ulysses*), not by leaning symbolically on his father. Writing and nomination are the substance of the *sinthome* that supplements the foreclosure of the Name-of-the-Father.

THE EGO

The *sinthome*—this symptom that knots the real, the symbolic, and the imaginary—is the singular invention of the subject, and more especially so in psychosis, since it does not use the "standard" of the Name-of-the-Father. The symptom of the child comes to "compensate" for the failure of his father. John Joyce, according to Lacan, taught his son nothing, sending him to the Jesuits for his education. For Joyce, the symptom of imposed speech will respond to this renunciation of paternity. In the following generation, Lucia responds to this deficiency of the father by prolonging her father's symptom of imposed speech by a gift of telepathy and schizophrenic "double vision." Lacan called Joyce's art a sinthome, thus designating a transformation of his initial symptom through his *savoir-faire* as an artist. Joyce's *œuvre* testifies to the fact that art (and not just analytic interpretation) can aim at what first presents itself as a symptom in order to thwart it. Joyce managed to avoid the evolution toward the madness to which Lucia succumbed, thanks to his work on the English language. From the infantile symptomatic kernel of imposed speech, a double movement sketches itself out in Joyce: defense and transmission. The movement of rejecting the invasion of imposed speech can be found in almost any passage of the *Portrait*.[44] The movement of transmission, which we have characterized as the attempt to write the voice, knots, as we have seen, the real and the symbolic in the epiphany. Lacan reads the "fault" of Joyce's knot in this, a fault that is correlative to the slipping of the imaginary ring, the clinical testimony of which Lacan sees in the second scene upon which we have commented above. Henceforth, the double movement continues to develop and accentuate itself: Joyce, through the intermediary of writing, decomposes the English language while letting it impose itself upon him. One cannot interpret his art as a simple defense against imposed speech, because it imposes itself more and more, to the point of dissolving language, as in *Finnegans Wake*. Imposed speech is received in order to be transmuted in writing.

Lacan's thesis bears upon another point, correlative to his own writing of Joyce's knot, which remains to be examined. Joyce's art, his *sinthome*, serves him as an ego. But how can a *sinthome* be an *ego*? The Lacanian *ego* is normally structured as an imaginary identification made at the mirror stage. Usually, Lacan uses the French term "*moi*." However, he preferred the term *ego* in 1951, at the time of his conference in London, and he uses it again in the *Sinthome* where he

---

44. "And it was the din of all these hollowsounding voices that made him halt irresolutely in the pursuit of phantoms. He gave them ear only for a time but he was happy only when he was far from them, beyond their call, alone or in the company of phantasmal comrades" (Joyce 1916, p. 87).

proposes to take up the question of the *ego* within the framework of his theory of knots. This is what he does for the case of Joyce by giving it a completely different sense to that of an identification with an image, with the image of the body:

> The idea of self as a body has a weight—it is what is called the ego. If the ego is said to be narcissistic, it is because at a certain level something supports the body as an image. However, in the case of Joyce, the fact is that, in the event, this image is not involved. Doesn't this ratify that for him the *ego* has a very particular function? [Session of March 16, 1976]

Indeed, faced with the aggression of the other, Joyce lets his body fall away like one drops an item of clothing. Thus the narcissistic relation of the subject with his body, namely "the idea of self as a body," in other words the *ego*, is not supported by an image.

However, the *ego* could be supported by his art. In what way can Joyce's art, his writing, be an *ego*? In what way does writing make his body hold together; in what way does it supply a point of support to the latter that would be different from an image? The *Portrait of the Artist as a Young Man*, which according to Aubert is the first truly Joycean work, is a text on the body. To write on the body permits Joyce not to identify with the image of his body, but to have a body (cf. Kaltenbeck 1999). This reveals that Joyce's "trouble" is closer to schizophrenia than paranoia, which supposes the image as a support. Let us note, for example, the importance of the theme of the "portrait" (1916): the imagination of his portrait as a Jesuit, portrait galleries, the title of the *Portrait* itself, and the importance of the successive frames in which the body is inscribed, in particular in *Ulysses*. Moreover, his friends are presented through a series reflections on their bodies or absence of bodies. Heron has a beak; Cranly has a face without body, two feminine eyes, a death mask,[45] then he finds his body again. Lynch is presented through his body: his "so muscular

---

45. "he saw it before him like the phantom of a dream, the face of a severed head or deathmask, crowned on the brows by its stiff black upright hair as by an iron crown" (Joyce 1916, p. 181).

frame . . . shook all over" (p. 205). As for Stephen-Joyce, he never
stops talking about his own, as: "drifting amid life like the barren
shell of the moon" (p. 98), "burning pulp" (p. 125), a "corpse" (p. 115),
"mortified" (p. 154), "aflame" (p. 176), "the mystery" (p. 173),
"plunging headlong through space" (p. 128), and so on. The soul is
conceived as a sort of double of the body. The soul is perhaps the name
of this "idea of self as a body," of this *ego* supported by writing.

Lacan uses three striking formulas in relation to Joyce: "to make
himself into a book" (Session of January 13, 1976), "to be an artist
who would occupy everyone" (Session of February 17, 1976), "to want
a name for himself" (ibid.). The last two imply the dimension of the
recognition accorded to the writer by his contemporaries and by subsequent generations, and the existence of a different kind of ideal-
ego than that of the mirror stage. The third evokes a nomination
which, as we have seen above, articulates with the *sinthome* insofar
as it supplements the foreclosure of the Name-of-the-Father. The first
responds to the question of "being." The question also poses itself
for Schreber: to be something other than the phallus for the mother,
in other words the woman, knowing that the phallus is foreclosed. It
is interesting to see that Lacan also says that the Joycean sinthome
supplements the foreclosure of the phallus: "And Joyce's art is what
truly answers for his phallus," "But as he had a bit of a loose prick, if
I may say so, it is his art which supplements his hold on his phallus,
and this is always the case."[46]

JOYCE'S KNOT WITH THE *SINTHOME*-EGO

The writing of Joyce's knot draws the consequences of the preceding
construction. At the level of the knot, Lacan represents the *ego* as a
fastening mechanism that stops the imaginary ring from slipping away,
as was the case in Figure 6–3. The *sinthome*-ego repairs the fault of
the knot (the knotting of the real and the symbolic) by reattaching
the real and the symbolic for a second time, thereby wedging the

---

46. *Le Sinthome*, op. cit., November 18, 1975.

imaginary (cf. figure in Session of May 11, 1976). Lacan's idea is that the *ego* (art) repairs the fault, not by taking something away but by redoubling it: it concerns a work of reflection, through writing, of the imposed speech that accentuates it, redoubling it in an effort that grew greater over time. What tends to slip away is the image of the body deducted from the mirror stage, while what secures the imaginary is, by contrast, the *ego* as the idea of the body constructed through writing.

(Translated by Philip Dravers)

REFERENCES

Aubert, J., ed. (1982). *James Joyce, Oeuvres I*, Bibliotheque de la Pleiade, NRF. Paris: Gallimard.

Aubert, J. (2000). D'un Joyce a l'autre. In *Lacan, l'ecrit, l'image*, ed. J. Aubert, F. Cheng, J.-C. Milner, et al., pp. 55–77. Paris: Champs Flammarion.

Ellmann, R. (1959). *James Joyce*. New York: Oxford University Press.

Freud, S. (1900). *The Interpretation of Dreams. Standard Edition* 4/5:1–338.

Joyce, J. (1916). *A Portrait of the Artist as a Young Man*. London: Paladin, 1988.

———— (1922). *Ulysses*. London: Penguin, 1986.

———— (1966). *Stephen Hero*. London: Four Square.

Kaltenbeck, F. (1999). Promenades avec Ulysses: huit leçons sur l'art de James Joyce. *Hors-Serie des Carnets de Lille*, L'atelier 3:5–62.

Lacan, J. (1966). *Ecrits: A Selection*. London: Tavistock/Routledge, 1977.

———— (1974–1975). Seminar XXII: *R.S.I. Ornicar? Periodique du Champ freudien*, nos. 3–5. Paris: Navarin.

———— (1975–1976). Seminar XXIII: *Le Sinthome. Ornicar? Periodique du Champ freudien*, nos. 6–11. Paris: Navarin.

Morel, G. (2000). *Ambiguites Sexuelle, Sexuation et Psychose*. Paris: Anthropos-Economica.

7

Art as Prosthesis: Cronenberg's Crash

PARVEEN ADAMS

I start with a quotation from Lacan's (1955–1956) seminar on Psychoses:

> Imagine a machine that has no mechanism for overall self-regulation, so that the organ designed to make the right leg walk was unable to coordinate with the one that makes the left leg walk unless a photo-electric receiver transmits the image of another machine functioning in a coordinated way. Think of these little automobiles that you see at fairs going round full tilt out in an open space, where the principal amusement is to bump into the others. If these dodg'em cars give so much pleasure, it is because bumping into one another must be something fundamental in the human being. What would happen if a certain number of little machines like those I describe were put on the track? Each one being unified and regulated by the sight of another, it is not mathematically impossible to imagine that we would end up with all the little machines accumulated in the center of the track, blocked in a conglomeration. . . . A collision, everything smashed to a pulp. [pp. 95–96]

This is a burlesque account of a psychotic world that might also seem to fit Cronenberg's film *Crash*. But when I first started to write about the film I felt defensive, for I had my own reasons for not wanting to read the film and its space in terms of psychosis.[47]

One of the things that people would expect to enter into the definition of normality is that subjects exist in three-dimensional space and in time. From the point of view of psychoanalysis, this three-dimensional world that is also temporal cannot be taken as an *a priori* condition of the subject; it has to be understood as a psychic construction. In Seminar XII (1964–1965), Lacan elucidates this point by arguing that the third dimension is an effect of the subject's identification in the field of the Other. Space is thus the effect of identification rather than the medium of identification. By contrast, the psychotic cannot make this identification and therefore cannot enter this space. Both the neurotic and the pervert can and do enter the field of the Other, but they do so differently. The neurotic does so as a subject, the pervert as an object. They can be globally distinguished from psychosis by the fact that they *complete* three-dimensional psychical space, at the same time as they can be distinguished from each other. Now my argument is that neither the cinematic nor the psychical space of *Crash* is three-dimensional. Yet if I try to sustain the idea that we are *not* dealing with psychosis, what kind of exceptional state are we dealing with here?

THE FAULT IN THE UNIVERSE

Perhaps we find a route to it in Lacan's writings of the mid-seventies, most crucially the seminar on the Sinthome (Lacan 1975–1976). It thinks about a subject who is not psychotic and yet is *not* bounded by castration and the paternal metaphor, a subject who is, as it were, outwith—that is, outside—the Other. It took some time to fully develop the idea of such a subject, one closely associated with a new concept of writing. For it is in the Sinthome seminar that Lacan de-

---

47. See Adams 2000.

velops his ideas on James Joyce and his extraordinary writing. Luke Thurston (1998), in his doctoral thesis on Lacan's Joycean knot, locates an early moment of this development in Lacan's changing conception of the barred subject. He writes: "By the 1960s it [the bar] stands for the subject's *inscription*, in a primal moment of identification or 'fixation,' in the real. Thus the subject's very foundation, the anchorage which prevents its dissolution in the flow of signification, is posited as a moment of *writing*."

This subject of inscription coexists with the subject of the signifier and it can do something that the subject of the signifier cannot do— it can sometimes come to authorize its own mark upon the world. This implies that the subject of inscription functions at the level of the Real, hence outwith the field of the Other. Certainly Lacan's view was that writing "fixed" Joyce in the Real and placed him outside the field of the Other. I had not understood all of this in my earlier analysis of the film. I had certainly argued that *Crash* reaches beyond representation and that the omnipresent scars of *Crash* were beyond the reach of any interpretation of castration. I had also identified the withdrawal from the field of the Other in purely cinematic terms. But I had refused to admit the analysis of psychosis while having no alternative path. Now I have the idea of the subject who authorizes his own mark on the world.

This clarifies my earlier insistence on the scar as pure inscription. Had the scar been the mark of castration it would indeed have opened onto metaphor and metonymy, bungled actions and bungled words, the poem, dreams and symptoms. In other words, castration would open the space of representation. The description involves the domain of the subject of the unconscious. But in *Crash* what is at stake is the *jouissance* of the scar as pure inscription, as a writing in the real that has none of these effects. For it is not the subject of the unconscious that is doing this writing. This writing is a writing in the real that has a link with art.

Lacan developed his argument about the subject outside the field of the Other through a new theory of the symptom that served as a means of thinking about the work of James Joyce. If my argument is to work, I must show how it might also serve as a means of thinking about *Crash*.

This has not done away with the problem of the relation to psychosis, for that now presents itself in an even stronger form. Lacan's analysis of Joyce identifies Joyce's nonsense writing as a solution to the problem of the collapse of the paternal function in his case. Remember that Lacan had originally sketched this collapse in his 1955–1956 seminar *The Psychoses*. He locates the problem of psychosis in the missing signifier of the Name-of-the-Father and the bypassing of the Oedipus complex. Even if in some sense the psychotic is in the Symbolic, the condition is characterized by a lack of phallic meaning and the lack of an orientation in the field of the Other. The fault lies in the relation of the psychotic subject to the Other.

A theoretical development was necessary to enable a distinction to be made between the subject in some relation to the Other and a subject outwith the Other. This didn't happen all at once. Quite early on, Lacan qualified the notion of the unbarred Other. There is a fault in the Other such that it is not complete and consistent. This is "the fault in the universe" that Lacan speaks of in 1973, but now it transforms the whole field since the topology of the 1970s is based on the barred Other. Now the relations between subject, object, and Other revolve around the fault in the universe. Where once Symbolic, Imaginary, and Real fell into place through the paternal metaphor, now the Other is not assumed and the rings of real, symbolic, and imaginary are disconnected to start with. Something extra is needed to supplement the fault, to tie the three orders together. Earlier this task fell to the Symbolic, but now it doesn't suffice. An admixture of *jouissance* is required to accomplish the task of knotting the orders together, and the symptom supplies it.

We could say that the introduction of the idea of the fault in the universe forces a certain generalization of foreclosure. It is not that we are all psychotics, but that the signifier that allows the quilting of signification is missing for all of us. The symptom, defined anew, now provides the necessary supplement that relates the three orders to one another. But the way in which it does this means that for all of us the signifier also continues to appear in the real. For the symptom is no longer metaphor. It no longer relates to the unconscious. The symptom is something that is added to the symbolic; it lies alongside the ring of the symbolic and yields a symbolic of a different kind. For there is a *jouissance* of the symptom and it plays outside the Other.

Lacan (1976) explained this at a conference in the United States in the mid-seventies. He said that the symptom Σ lies in a circle with the unconscious and that once the circle of the symbolic is both S and Σ, "that makes a new kind of S" (p. 58). So there are two sides of the new symbolic—on the one hand the signifier that enters into a relation with another signifier and forms a chain, and on the other, the letter. Pierre Skriabine (1993) notes that J.-A. Miller, apropos of the signifier, spoke of the function of representation on the one hand and the function of the symptom on the other.

The symptom can no longer be thought of as expressed by the logic of the unconscious alone, as that which belongs to the realm of sense and the symbolic. Insofar as there is now a general theory of the symptom, it partakes of the *jouissance* of the letter. So the signifier sustains the function of the symptom as well as that of representation. Paradoxically it is the symptom that allows entry into the signifying chain. Skriabine describes ". . . the mythical moment when the subject, in the Other where he is spoken, recognises himself in an S1—a mark, a letter, that which guarantees the essential function of the symptom; which in turn, as symbolic nomination, is a name-of-the-father in its place as fourth [i.e., in the knot]. (p. 133)

Importantly this coordination of *jouissance* and meaning applies in the case of both neurotic and psychotic. What Lacan has done is to turn the Name-of-the-Father into the symptom that ties the three registers together. But does this account for the *jouissance* of Joyce, the *sinthome*? The answer is no, and this requires that the symptom and the *sinthome* be differentiated. For here the fourth ring does not lie in a circle with the unconscious, and the Joycean solution does not rectify this. In his case the *sinthome* is produced at that point where the knotting failed, where the imaginary slid away, leaving the symbolic and the real knotted together.[48] Precisely there, the Joycean *ego* comes as a second tying of the real and symbolic in such a way as to include the imaginary and tie the R.S.I. knot. But with the ego as the fourth ring, the knot is skewed. The ego that produces the skewed knot is the *sinthome*, and it carries the memory of the original fault. Skriabine quotes Lacan to show that the construction of the Joycean ego is a minimal way of repairing the fault. The ego constitutes a pure symptom "that Joyce succeeds in raising to the power of language, without, for all that, anything being analyzable" (Skriabine 1993, p. 131). This symptom does not lie in a circle with the unconscious. The fourth ring of the ego does not introduce meaning, the unconscious, or the Other.

Luke Thurston (1998) gives a rich and resonating account of the difference of the Joycean knot:

> Joyce's knot is not "really" Borromean: it is not tied properly, to form a balanced, ordered interrelation of real, symbolic, and imaginary, but is drastically "skewed" by its reliance on the *sinthome* for coherence. The movement and "play" of the Borromean knot, which for Lacan is the topological equivalent of the subject as a space of signifying displacement, is radically hampered by the "prosthetic" fourth register in Joyce, which bolts in place the "subject" as "aspace of dumbillsilly." [chapter III, section 4]

This bolting in place of the subject accounts for the solitary *jouissance* of Joyce and that is what distinguishes it from the *jouissance* of the psychotic, as we will see.

The generalization of foreclosure inherent in the idea of the R.S.I. knot does not blur clinical differences. It clearly matters whether the fourth ring is the Name-of-the-Father as in the case of the neurotic or the ego as in the case of Joyce. But now the lack of the paternal

---

48. This account suggests that we are not dealing with the usual Borromean knot where a cut would result in the untying of all three rings. Nonetheless we must suppose that Real, Imaginary, and Symbolic hang together in some way before the Joycean solution is put in place. However, the original knotting is faulty, as the moments of epiphany show.

metaphor and the disturbance of the imaginary can be found everywhere, though it is taken up differently in different cases. There are
all sorts of combinations and relations. Previously mutually exclusive definitions have been diluted in a new synthesis. Now we find a
variety of seemingly similar problems together with a host of different solutions.

Let me emphasize that what counts as a solution for the subject
has changed with the formulation of the fault in the universe. The
symptom itself is the solution; the symptom is the *name* of the subject's
relation to the fault in the universe. We now have a new kind of symptom, the necessary symptom. Far from ridding ourselves of the symptom, we must construct it. Since we have to tolerate the symptom,
we should construct it as adeptly as possible.

My revised analysis of *Crash* draws upon the knowledge that the
separation of the three rings of the symbolic, the imaginary, and the
real is a situation with the possibility of different solutions. Certainly
Crash had looked like the catastrophic world of the psychotic, and
indeed it shares many of its characteristics. The question now is what
kind of symptom are we dealing with—psychotic symptom or Joycean
sinthome?[49]

JOYCE, THE SINTHOME

Lacan analyzes Joyce without him, just as Freud analyzed Schreber.
Schreber and Joyce helped themselves without Freud and Lacan.
Colette Soler (1993) puts the difference succinctly. Schreber is "a case
of self-cure, outside the transference. As for Joyce, that would be rather
a case of auto-prevention of the illness" (p. 51). But what is the basis
for the comparison? It is that they share the enigmatic experience that
is an effect of the signifier. Soler clarifies the point, "there . . . where

---

49. It is unclear whether we are to take symptom and sinthome as equivalent.
I would prefer to reserve the term *sinthome* to refer to that form of symptom that
comes close to the identification with the symptom that is supposed to take place at
the end of analysis.

. . . the lack was, the void of signification, that is, quite simply, the impossibility of responding to the question: 'What does that signify?' there, there comes that which is not of emptiness but of certitude, inherent to the signifier, that that signifies" (p. 52). Failure to answer the question only strengthens the conviction that there is an answer.

Soler also describes a difference in the way the enigmatic is experienced by Schreber and by Joyce. For the former it comes about as hallucination, for the latter through the experience of what Joyce called epiphany. The simultaneous experience of the enigmatic void and vivid certitude *is* the experience of epiphany. In *Stephen Hero* Joyce (1955) writes, "By epiphany he meant a sudden spiritual manifestation, whether in the vulgarity of speech or of gesture or in a memorable phase of the mind itself" (p. 216). However apparently trivial, the enigmatic is of the utmost significance for Joyce, which relates as the *name* of his vocation. Catherine Millot (1987) writes of this Joycean epiphany that on the one hand it is "something empty, of a perfectly futile, fleeting, inconsistent sense, and on the other an absolute density of meaning, ineffable, intransmissable, completely enigmatic, on which Joyce founds the certitude of his vocation" (p. 91).

Lacan links the Joycean epiphany with the failure of the function of the ego. Let me elaborate on this way of understanding the problem of Joyce's existence through an example. It is an incident taken from the early novel *A Portrait of the Artist as a Young Man*. It describes the occasion when Stephen (Joyce) gets a thorough thrashing from his school friends after a discussion of heresy, and it is Stephen's response that Lacan emphasizes. On remembering this scene he noted, "the memory of it called forth no anger from him. . . . Even that night when he stumbled homeward along Jones's Road, he had felt that some power was divesting him of that sudden woven anger as easily as a fruit is divested of its soft ripe peel" (Joyce 1916, p. 114). We are talking about a dislocation of the image of the body, a disturbance in the mirror stage. The ring of the imaginary has slipped out of the knot that it should have formed with the real and the symbolic.

There is another example from the *Portrait*, which makes clear Stephen's way of dealing with the problem. It concerns the fetus. Stephen's father had taken him to his old college, Queen's, where, with the help of the porter, he seeks his initials in the anatomy theater. Stephen remains in the background, but "On the desk he read the word *Foetus* cut several times in the dark stained wood. The sudden legend startled his blood. . . ." Walking back with his father,

> He could scarcely recognise as his his own thoughts, and repeated slowly to himself: I am Stephen Dedalus. I am walking beside my father whose name is Simon Dedalus. We are in Cork, in Ireland. Cork is a city. Our room is in the Victoria Hotel. Victoria and Stephen and Simon. Simon and Stephen and Victoria. Names.
>
> 　The memory of his childhood suddenly grew dim. He tried to call forth some of its vivid moments but could not. He recalled only names. Dante, Parnell, Clane, Clongowes. [p. 122]

The story includes the father, who is always portrayed as failing in his function; the foetus, that is Stephen himself in a nonsymbolic form, not yet having acceded to subjecthood; and the desperate holding onto names when meaning fails. And what is a name? It is the signifier in its aspect of the letter, of the mark that carries *jouissance* into the very heart of the symbolic. Stephen holds onto symbolic and real when confronted by the apparition of the foetus. This marks but doesn't resolve the problem of the nonexistence of the subject. Joyce, Lacan says, will construct his ego and will weave an existence for himself through *écriture*, a writing in the real.

Paradoxically, écriture involves a repetition of the failure of the paternal relation. The solution comes about through a repetition of failure! So you begin to see why the new idea of the ego that Lacan was elaborating feels strange. Joyce has claimed that both in *Ulysses* and in *Finnegans Wake* he used the material of conversations from everyday life, that is to say he repeats what he has heard. In so doing he makes meaning quite unimportant, opening up, as he does, a gap between the enunciation and the enounced. Now in the *Portrait*, just such a gap exists for Stephen. He listens to what his father is saying to him and repeats the words he does not understand. For Stephen, the father is the voice of the father. Joyce listens to voices in the everyday places of his daily life and without relating to what is being said he uses what he has heard in his work. This relation of repetition is a hallmark of his art. He could only respond to whatever it was that his father's words did to him, by repeating them. And yet Lacan says that this very repetition enables the building of an ego that allows a knotting of the three registers that had come apart.

THE JOYCEAN SOLUTION

Joyce's art consists of the kind of repetition that can only be described as the repetition of the failure of the paternal relation. And yet Lacan says that this very repetition enables the building of an ego that allows a knotting of the three registers that had come apart.

A quotation from *Ulysses* comes to the support of Lacan's theory here.

> as we . . . weave and unweave our bodies, Stephen said, from day to day, their molecules shuttled to and fro, so does the artist weave and unweave his image. And as the mole on my right breast is where it was when I was born, though all my body has been woven of new stuff time after time, so through the ghost of the unquiet father the image of the unliving son looks forth. In the intense instant of imagination, when the mind, Shelley says, is a fading coal, that which I was is that which I am and that which in possibility I may come to be. [Joyce 1937, p. 183]

The Joycean I, ego, is there at the moment of creation. So the solution lies in the constant weaving and unweaving in the moments of creation. The ego is constructed at the level of the real. Now we can see what makes this ego so radically different—it has nothing to do with the unconscious. Joyce does not help himself with the help of the unconscious. You can see that we have left behind the world of psychoanalysis and the oedipal law. Lacan claims "that Joyce succeeds in raising [the ego] to the power of language, without, for all that, anything being analysable."

We can return to the justification of the difference of the *sinthome*. Consider the psychotic who attempts to supplement the fault in the universe through the metaphors of delirium that try to localize *jouissance*. What the psychotic is doing is putting in place a supplement for the missing supplement of the Name-of-the-Father. The delirious metaphor takes the place of the paternal one. Then consider the symptom not as delirium but as letter saturated with *jouissance*. This is what is special in Joyce. He acts in the knowledge that the Other is barred and deals with the fault in the universe *in his own way*.

That idea of the fault in the universe allows us to highlight *jouissance* in the new definition of the symptom. It is the way of dealing with the category of *jouissance* that is at stake, once the idea of foreclosure is generalized. The distinction between symptom and *sinthome* has to do with the way in which the rings of the R.S.I. are reknotted and hence with the way in which *jouissance* is handled. Lacan takes us beyond the idea of *jouis-sens*, enjoyment in the production of meaning, something we might think of as the limit of analytic discourse, toward an idea of a solitary *jouissance* outside the Other, the *jouissance* of the sinthome.

Joyce puts his symptom in place by writing the *jouissance* of the signifier.

CRASH AND THE *JOUISSANCE* OF THE SINTHOME

I had originally said that castration is vanquished by inscription in that landscape of battered metal and pink flesh that Cronenberg presents to us. I now do think that *Crash* has something of what Lacan attributes to Joyce, especially around the question of the subject of inscription and the possibility of forging one's own identity in facing the knowledge that the Other does not exist. There are parallels both with the experience of epiphany and with what Lacan calls the "artifice d'écriture" (Lacan 1975–1976, Session of May 11, p. 8). That one belongs to literature and the other to cinema does not matter, though the mechanism of the play with *lalangue* that Lacan isolates is specific, of course, to Joyce. Since *Crash* does not unfold as language, I will have to identify what it is that takes the place of écriture.

Something of the experience of epiphany is found in *Crash*, which, if not at the level of language, is at the level of Joyce's response to the thrashing he received. Lacan concluded from the account of this incident that Joyce had let go of the relation to his body. It may be paradoxical but I claim that in this film full of bodies and sex, the characters do not live in their bodies either. The bodies in *Crash* are certainly strange, and this is especially true of Catherine. Are these not "voided"/ "emptied out"/"peeled" bodies? No two characters are face to face. Catherine, in the early scene with Ballard on the balcony of their apartment, high up over the highway, is staring straight ahead. Not "ahead" as a direction but "ahead" as what lies on the other side of the windscreen. She speaks, but is elsewhere. The characters are never together, even fucking.

The epiphany revolves around enigmatic meaning. For Joyce, the drama of the emptying out of meaning occurs at the same moment as the insistence that this really has a meaning, a moment at which lack and plenitude appear as one. In *Crash*, this role is played by the car crashes. The significance of the crash is reduced and emptied out, not only by the film but by us. We normally call them accidents, as though what happens every day is dissociated from the order of the structure. But the crash, if not this one then the next one, is the film's real order. One survives the crash only by accident. One outlives the Other by waiting for the crash. Or to use the Scot's legal term, one is outwith the Other.

If this is the epiphany in *Crash*, it is still necessary to elaborate the forms of the collapse of the imaginary in *Crash* more specifically. Here I think the analysis of André Gide by Lacan (1966), nearly twenty years before that of Joyce, is helpful. For Lacan, Gide was also characterized by a disturbance in the imaginary. But it was not at all the case that this was anything like Joyce's epiphanies. In his 1988 seminar Miller has commented closely on Lacan's argument, which means that the later ideas of Lacan, in particular the generalization of foreclosure, informs the commentary (Miller 1993). Lacan discusses the nature of Gide in terms of the mother in whom the functions of love and desire have become dissociated. What happens to the son of such a dissociation? Inevitably he reproduces it. Lacan argues that since she had not desired the phallus in her husband or in her son, little Gide had not been a phallicized child.

From the point of view of desire, the mother was responsible for the mortification of the phallus. Put in terms of the unconscious, there is a desire for a dead phallus. This is quite different from castration. Lacan assigns the child a place "between death and masturbatory erotism." There is a mortification of the phallic signifier and so Gide cannot identify with his "*être de vivant*" (Miller 1993, p. 27), his living being. He identifies instead with his "*être de mort*," his being of death. Gide is therefore not a subject inscribed under the phallic signifier.

But the absence of phallic signification must provoke some disturbance in the imaginary order. Miller draws out Lacan's point about what Gide himself described as a "trembling" in the depths of his being. He feels excluded from the relation to the semblable and says, "I am not like the others." There is no relation to the other.

For Gide, the lack of a relation to the other stemming from the failure of the paternal metaphor leads to what Lacan calls *the trait of the cadaver*. Gide's love object must meet a condition: it must signify death. Even more, the object itself must be so split that the shadow of death falls on it. This splitting (or doubling) is at the level of the imaginary and is also to be found in that famous case of psychosis, Schreber. Miller claims that this doubling is found when the paternal metaphor fails. And given that the paternal metaphor itself is never perfectly inscribed, such doubling is to be found in neurotics as well. Miller (1993) writes, "The duplication of the object . . . allows the very precise marking of the malfunctioning of the paternal metaphor. It is the imaginary index, immediately perceptible, which must be read in a double way: at the level of the imaginary, and at the properly symbolic level, where it has its determinants" (p. 31).

This doubling, to be found everywhere as Miller indicates, does not itself determine the course of desire. Perhaps the palpable presence of doubling indicates something of the scale of the disturbance. Yet it is the character of desire that yields the particularity of a case. Normally love and desire would tend to converge. This is not so for

Gide for whom love goes with death, and the condition of love and choice of object is the trait of the cadaver. The mother of love, the mortification of the phallus, the preeminence of death, are all themes that make it impossible to even conceive of the origin and destiny of desire in such a being. Miller concurs in the solution that for a subject who has not been phallicized, desire must come from the outside: "It is because we have the negative incidence on the one side, that *desire in its positivity comes from the outside as a violent intrusion*" (p. 32).

It seems to me that the themes—the lack of the relation to the other, the trait of the cadaver, the violent intrusion of desire—constitute a series whose application extends well beyond the fictitious case history of Gide. I will try to show how they have a reference in *Crash*, at the level of clarifying its lack of phallic signification and therefore its disturbance of the imaginary. If I can show that the imaginary has come adrift in *Crash*, it will also serve to answer those who say that *Crash* is about the problem of frigidity.

The lack of relation to the other in *Crash* is established through a kind of doubling, that of coupling. The film obliterates any difference between homosexual and heterosexual sex. But this difference, indeed difference in general, is the detail that sustains the three-dimensionality of the world in general. The indifferent coupling redraws the boundaries of participants so that the situation can be expressed as a solitary relation. It seems to reflect a generalization of Gide's condition, down to the claim that Gide's *jouissance* remained masturbatory.

The trait of the cadaver itself requires a doubling of the object. The object divides itself: the body is doubled by all the signs of death that cast their shadow back upon the body. One does not read the scars as an optimistic testimony to medical prowess. They are signs of a death postponed, a death rehearsal, a death-in-waiting. So profound is the economy of doubling, of the movement from one to two, that it precisely describes the move from suture to wound, the opening of the scar, the splitting of the scar into a wound. In *Crash*, the scar is the trait of the cadaver. Just think of Gabriella's body. The scar signifies an accident, hopefully a fatal one. This is established through the film's primal scene, that early scene where Ballard kills Helen's husband. Both Helen and Ballard earn their scars from this accident.

This trait of the cadaver is doubled, in the sense that the scar is not only a rehearsal for death but also refers to a prior death.

In *Crash* the relation between accident and structure is the reverse of any existentialist use of the car as a way of introducing death as a possible outcome. In *Rebel Without A Cause* the game of chicken is used to enable the danger of an accident to re-eroticize the structure of life. It is an adventure for bored boys. By contrast, in *Crash*, as the title suggests, the accident lies not on the side of death but of survival. Any eroticism that is left over to me in the period before my death is lent to me only by the generosity of my dead body, which is guaranteed by the structure of these crashes. These are no accident and they will produce, if not this time then the next time, the dead body that is the object of my *jouissance*.

This situation reverses the normal relations of accident and structure. This effect is not simply at the level of the narrative of *Crash* but points to a further consequence. *The eroticism of the structure of crashing comes from outside the structure of the subject*; from the usual point of view of the subject, crashes come not as a structure but as an accident. In *Rebel Without a Cause*, whether the chicken player survives or dies, it is the subject's relation to that event that is at stake. Here the subject constitutes a kind of interiority faced with the external causality embodied in the car. Either he survives and his desire is reanimated, or he dies and it is a tragic loss for his peers. Desire and tragedy are different outcomes for the interior life of the subject.

But in *Crash*, the structure is on the outside. What is accidental in this case is the survival of the subject. The erotic structure relates simply to the suspense of waiting to die, of the violence that characterizes the transition from having a wound to being a wound. The rigor and grasp of this erotic economy is evidenced by the fact that all orifices of the participants are always already wounds from the beginning. The final violence, which is in a way mimicked by the humans' relation to machinery, is that the violence constitutes no authentic unfolding of the subject's interiority. This economy can settle on any unsuspecting driver. What is most destituting for human intelligence is that the mechanism of this crash has no causality. It belongs at the edge of a pure exteriority.

We appear to have landed somewhere outside the territory that Gide inhabits. For *Crash* raises the idea of a violent intrusion of desire from the outside to a higher power. Crash takes us into a space quite outside the Other. What does this imply at the level of the three rings that usually tie to yield the R.S.I. knot? Remember that in the 1970s the account of structure did not take the Other as a given. The Other is an effect of the knotting. It looks as though *Crash* has tied the knot in such a way as to withdraw from the field of the Other. This, of course, is what Joyce did.

How does *Crash* visualize for the viewer the space outside the Other? What do we see when we watch the film? A first response to the question is that the viewer sees the flatness of the surface of the film. The mechanisms that usually construct a field of enunciation in film are no longer in place. Doors, windows, flashbacks, voiceovers, and so on, all those reflexive mechanisms that Christian Metz identified as producing filmic space, are absent. *Crash* confronts us with the collapse of three-dimensional space (cf. Adams 2000).

But there is more to it than that. This collapse is not only cinematic but psychical at the same time. For not only is filmic depth reduced to a layer, but the viewer, too, experiences a spatial reduction. Lacan claims that the three-dimensionality of the subject is achieved only by entering the field of the Other. So the subject's relation to space is bound up with the subject's relation to the Other. If the viewer *sees* differently in *Crash* it has to do with the change in the three-dimensionality of the scene. This flattens *him* by making him lose his psychical coordinates. He ends up not knowing at all where he is. I am suggesting that this collapse of space at the pictorial level is equivalent to the collapse of sense at the linguistic level in the case of Joyce. The viewer of *Crash* is outwith the Other.

Let me put all this in the dominant terms of Lacan's seminar. Using Miller's account of Gide, I have argued that there is a collapse of the imaginary in *Crash*, the solution to which is of the order of the sinthome. For *Crash* equips the spectator with a prosthetic ego. If Joyce constructs his ego through a repetition of failure, so does *Crash*, both at the level of narrative and at the level of the collapse of the enunciative field. The spectator deals with a problem not of his own making in a manner that bolts him into an uncomfortable space of *jouissance*.

So the supplement in *Crash* is not the psychotic symptom but the Joycean sinthome. In *Crash* it is the viewer who provides the supplement. And the knot of the Real, the Symbolic, and the Imaginary is tied in such a way that, as in the écriture of Joyce, it bolts the subject in place.

REFERENCES

Adams, P. (2000). Death drive. In *The Modern Fantastic: The Films of David Cronenberg*, ed. M. Grant, pp. 102–122. Trowbridge, UK: Flicks Books.

Joyce, J. (1916). *A Portrait of the Artist as a Young Man*. In *The Essential James Joyce*, ed. H. Levin, pp. 51–252. Harmondsworth, UK: Penguin, 1963.

—— (1937). *Ulysses*. London: Penguin, 1986.

—— (1939). *Finnegans Wake*. Harmondsworth, UK: Penguin, 1992.

—— (1955). *Stephen Hero*, ed. T. Spencer, J. J. Slocum, and H. Cahoon. London: Cape, 1969.

Lacan, J. (1955–1956). Seminar III: *The Psychoses*. London: Routledge, 1993.

—— (1964–1965). Seminar XII: *Problemes Cruciaux Pour la Psychanalyse*. Unpublished.

—— (1966). Jeunesse du Gide ou la lettre et le desir. In *Ecrits*, pp. 739–764. Paris: Seuil.

—— (1973). L'Etourdit. *Scilicet* 4:5–52.

—— (1975–1976). Seminar XXIII: *Le Sinthome*. *Ornicar? Periodique du Champ freudien*, nos. 6–11.

—— (1976). Conferences et Entretiens à MIT 1975. *Scilicet* 6/7:5–63.

Miller, J-A. (1993). Sur le Gide de Lacan. *La Cause Freudienne* (Critique de la Sublimation) 25:7–38.

Millot, C. (1987). Epiphanies. In *Joyce avec Lacan*, ed. J. Aubert, pp. 87–95. Paris: Navarin.

Skriabine, P. (1993). Clinique et topologie (deuxieme partie). *La Cause Freudienne* (L'Enigme et la Psychose) 23:127–133.

Soler, C. (1993). L'experience enigmatique du psychotique, De Schreber à Joyce. *La Cause Freudienne* (L'Enigme et la Psychose) 23:50–59.

Thurston, L. (1998). *Writing the Symptom: Lacan's Joycean Knot*. Doctoral thesis, University of Kent, Canterbury, UK. Unpublished.

8

"Se faire être une photographie":
The Work of Joel-Peter Witkin

PARVEEN ADAMS

"I am the work that I help to create," says Joel-Peter Witkin (1987, p. 15). These words are to be taken literally. Joel-Peter Witkin doesn't just make photographs; he makes photographs of himself. But this doesn't mean that he makes self-portraits. It is that in making the work he makes himself. Indeed he is interested in photography only insofar as it is about him. "I am not interested in photography per se, I am dedicating myself to myself. This is my vocation" (quoted in Celant 1995, pp. 24–25). My understanding of Witkin, which is in general consonant with his own, rests on Lacan's late writings on James Joyce. According to Lacan, it is Joyce who makes himself into a book ("*se faire être un livre*"). A book and a photograph are not the same thing, but if you are familiar with the 1975 seminar on Joyce, you might guess the direction my analysis will take. It concerns an unfamiliar and radical transformation of our idea of human beings.

What is familiar is Witkin's use of dead fetuses and fragments of cadavers, of live dwarves, preoperative transsexuals, those born with horns, wings, tails, or flippers, those with elephantine limbs, and so on. Three examples: the first, *The Kiss*, 1982, is of a head split in half

for an anatomy course; the second, *Portrait of a Dwarf*, 1987. Eugenia
Parry (1998) describes it: "An adorable dwarf who played E. T. in
Spielberg's film poses with the confident gaze of self-love in a satin mask
and lace camisole" (p. 181). The third example, *Las Meninas*, 1987, is
of a legless cripple atop a bare frame on wheels. According to Janis, the
preparatory drawing for this picture is entitled *Me, Crippled*.

What is going on with such an identification? How is Witkin
crippled? What sets him aside from others? Of course, we rely on his
own account of the matter, an early account made in his student days
in New Mexico. He tells the story of what befell him at the tender age
of 6. He is leaving the tenement he lives in with his mother and
brother, and they hear a terrible sound of a crash and screams and
cries for help. The accident had involved three families in cars. Witkin
writes: "At the place where I stood at the curb, I could see something
rolling from one of the overturned cars. It stopped at the curb where
I stood. It was the head of a little girl. I bent down to touch the face,
to ask it—but before I could touch it—someone carried me away"
(quoted in Celant 1995, p. 49).

Witkin will understand this as the primal scene of his work. As
Witkin bends down to address the head of the girl, to question her,
she is for him both alive and dead. And while it is a question of her
body, at the same time its pieces are flung in different directions. There
is no longer a boundary separating her from the world. If you don't
differentiate inside and outside, you don't exist. That head that rolled
to the curb shattered the proper image of Joel-Peter Witkin's body
and put his existence in question. Witkin is not explicit about the
disturbance in terms of the relation to the image of his body but he is
quite explicit about its effect: "I was confused by life, by its origination, continuation, and termination" (quoted in Celant 1995, p. 55).
It is as though *he* were the victim of the accident. So, Witkin Crippled.

Through his work Witkin comes to have the feeling of having
individual existence. He is clear about this, though he says that "that is
not exhaustively describable nor for that matter understandable." With
a little help from Lacan, *we* will understand how that is possible.

But before we get to that, we should know something about
Witkin's methods of work. I quote from Germano Celant's (1995) text:

Witkin uses an inordinately tactile photography, one capable of creating a corporeal dimension in which images seem to spout. . . . The very surfaces of his photographs thus return to epidermal values. It is almost as though their skin . . . this skin, site of the uncontrollable manifestations of existence, terrain of eroticism as well as necrophilia, is a threshold between outside and inside, between silence and screams, calm and violence. This is why it is often gouged with scratches and marks, both positive and negative, and printed through tissue paper onto Portiga paper using various chemicals to achieve different tones and layerings. Finally, with the camera obscura this skin is aged . . . assuming as it were the tactility of an image having arisen from the earth. At times the images are subjected to an encaustic process. After the print is archivally mounted on aluminium . . . Cynthia . . . hand tones the grains of the photographic surface with pigments. This process alone may take weeks to complete. Then the Witkins layer the print in pure molten beeswax and proceed to . . . [locally reheat the wax again to a liquid state]. The surface is then allowed to cool for several days, then polished by hand.

Through all these processes, the emulsified surface for the artist becomes the membrane on which the vibrations and impulses, the uncertainties and indecisions of a new life are registered. The photography is porous, impermeable, the seat of a deep perception at once physical and spiritual. *It possesses the image and is possessed by it* (my italics). In this sense it approaches painting, merging with the artist's inner gaze; *it is a piece of his skin which comes into being* (my italics), grows, moving about like a living thing. [p. 12]

We can now hazard a guess as to how it is that Witkin comes to feel that he has "an individual existence." Witkin suffers a disturbance in the imaginary, a disturbance that involves his relation to the *image* of his own body. I suggest that he makes up for this by constructing not an image but an *ego* through his picture-making. This idea derives from Lacan's work on Joyce. Lacan writes about the disturbance in the imaginary in Joyce and about the way in which his writing builds a substitute imaginary in the form of the ego. Of course, this is no ordinary kind of writing. Lacan calls it *écriture* and it is characterized as a writing in the real. That is to say, here signification is beside the point; what counts is the *jouissance* of the mark. So we have a texture of writing that *comes to be* the ego that Joyce lacks. It is in this way that Joyce makes himself into a book. You can appreciate that this is no ordinary kind of ego. Similarly, Witkin's construction of a photographic skin allows Witkin to make himself into a photograph. This skin is not of the order of the image of the mirror stage, though the picture is Witkin's ego. I will develop the idea of this ego as real later.[50]

So Witkin feels better making pictures. But he still suffers. What can be said about the viewer? The pictures have a rawness about them. I think this can be explained through both sides of the distinction I have just made between image and ego. The image retains and conveys the problem; the photographic surface serves as its solution. But while the solution is not altogether successful for Witkin himself insofar as he continues to suffer, for the viewer it generates a new problem. Now the photographic skin is yours and you find yourself trapped in your new ego, confined to a narrow, prosthetic space. *Jouissance* is seldom very nice, even when it is the solution to a problem.

Normally we would expect art to have the function of transforming *jouissance*, of bringing it under the regulation of the symbolic and the imaginary. Here we are dealing with a *jouissance* that has indeed been altered in some way, but that stubbornly remains outside meaning. Witkin devises an existence for himself through the making of the picture and simultaneously the problem of existence remains part of the picture. It is as though he had caught and trapped the problem into the frame of the picture. This gives him a degree of control but leaves us at the mercy of the picture.

To describe more precisely the uncomfortable space of Witkin's pictures, I return to Celant's (1995) text:

---

50. Witkin literally "stages" his scenes and sitters before photographing them. He uses drapes, frames, backdrops, and so on. Most striking is the way in which he transforms the sitter's body, not just with masks, but with the addition of lumps of fat, dentures, penile prostheses, etc. The artificiality of the staging is reminiscent of the perverse scenario. See Kaltenbeck, this volume, for the similarities and differences between perversion and the sinthome.

The quality conferred by encaustic and impasti of soil projects a petrified sense . . . in a terrible discovery, in which everything is transformed into relic and thing, into an unfathomable silence where the crust of the cosmos ceases to breathe as a life-substance. Here earth and mud are not regenerative, but serve rather to fix and seal. They enter the photograph's body like a tomb. . . . If the language of the images represents a return to the earth, it also documents a descent into Hell, into Hades, where it frees the dead and brings them back into circulation. [p. 13]

Celant is noting the effects of the skin of the picture, that skin that I have identified as the Witkinian ego. That it is the space of the tomb doesn't detract from its function. It does, however, emphasize this ego's restricted space and its separation from the world. Somewhere Witkin speaks of making enclosures. Of course, the womb is also an enclosure. Witkin is concerned, precisely, with both life and death. But he can only deal with their similarity and their difference in the special space he constructs in his pictures. The relation between life and death and the question of his own being is addressed in and through that space. It is a space not organized by the symbolic. The construction of the photographic skin has nothing to do with the Other. The entry into the field of the Other is necessary to the construction of our familiar habitual three-dimensional space, but Witkin has not entered that field and psychically speaking he does not inhabit three-dimensional space. The photographic skin, the ego, signals a space that has no depth. It is a space that is best described as a thick surface.

Let us take a moment to consider the technical means whereby Witkin achieves his effects. His labor over the photographs ensures the flatness of the represented space, the enclosure of space, and the transformation and congealing of light into something substantial. With no space and no light, you would indeed be in the tomb. One way in which Witkin suggests enclosure is by the use of what we may call "the aura." Many pictures are framed by a shaped space. In *Leda* (1986), there are several sources of light but it is the one from above that gives "the aura" that encompasses the entire picture. The strangeness of Witkin's pictures owes something to this kind of hollowing out of representational space. *The Kiss* (1982) comes immediately to mind.

As does the amazing *Feast of Fools* (1990), a picture after the manner of a seventeenth-century Dutch still life but with a difference, since amid the crustacea and the fruit lie hands, feet, and the head of a fetus. This is a self-contained space within its "aura." With the frontal lighting, it is almost as though our looking lights up the picture. There is no sense of an outside.

The sense of enclosure of the pictures is often reinforced through a device of repetition. In *Leda*, the shape of her figure is repeated in the scratched "shadows" on the left of the picture in such a way as to suggest that the picture might fold onto itself. In *Feast of Fools* there are two kinds of repetition: first, the shapes around the upper and lower edges that echo the forms of the still life, the hands, the feet, the octopus, and the fruit; second, the echoes within the still life ensemble—the cuts in the fruit, the insides of the fruit, the hand that grasps the tentacles of the octopus.

In *Woman in the Blue Hat* (1985), the flattening effect is to the fore. The woman is seated against a crudely painted backdrop. On the left is a rich curtain brightly lit from the right. The woman is lit from the left and you can see the dark stain of her shadow. The texture and shape of the hat is repeated in the foliage and in the clouds. Her forehead is a triangle of light—it is almost as if you can see through to the sky behind. It also matches the oblong of white just behind her left arm, and the white of that is the same as that of her bodice—a considerable flattening effect.

Similarly, the picture *Woman on a Table* (1987): there is the ground and then what should be a receding space enclosed by trees, but the picture is quite flat. The ground has become part of a picture on an easel. The picture is that of the woman (on a flat plane). The tree trunk on the right appears as the edge of the picture on the easel—the light on the trunk at its lowest point reinforces this. The woman is part of the picture inside the picture and yet throws a shadow on the ground in front of it. The larger picture marks the edge of space—it doesn't extend further in any direction.

Woman on a Table also illustrates the way in which light becomes object. It is lit from the left, so the shadow of the woman is thrown to the right of the table. But this shadow is not sharp, unlike the shadow of the table legs. It has become quite like other parts of the picture inside the picture. It has become substance. This picture, too, is in a space of its own, even though it has a source of light outside itself. For we could think of this source as of the sun over a landscape and paradoxically no sense of outside.

With *Las Meninas* (1987), we find something more akin to representational space. There is a middle ground with the table leg, its covering cloth, and some strange, small object connected to a wire on the ground. There is also a definite left side to the picture that is partially organized by the half frame of the well-lit picture of the king and queen. But with the Christ figure in the doorway, beyond which there is a dazzling light, it is as though we were looking out of the tomb at the world beyond. It is in *Las Meninas* that you see most clearly how light itself has been made into an object. The light shade on the right has been painted in the form of light rays, and this shape is then repeated as a "shadow" on a larger scale.

But if Witkin entombs himself, how can that help with the problem of the nonexistence of the subject? The answer lies in the ego that Witkin constructs through his art. For it is this ego that allows him the status of subject. The very activity that produces the spatial effects of the tomb also builds the ego. Of course, the latter does not necessarily produce effects of the tomb. But it is important in Witkin and explains something of the rawness of the pictures. Consider the real dead fetus in the picture. In a sense it is Joel-Peter Witkin himself, for the fetus is the being of the subject in a non-symbolic form.[51] The fetus in the space of the tomb retains the stark horror of the thing. At the same time, Witkin manages to accede to subjecthood by constructing his ego as photographic skin. It is clear how it can be that

---

51. See Geneviève Morel, this volume.

the solution does not do away with the *jouissance* it operated upon.
The solution organizes *jouissance* minimally, for this ego is outside
the symbolic.

I gave you Germano Celant's account of how Witkin labors to
construct his photographic skin. I suggest that it is something quite
distinct in art. Is it possible to liken this photographic skin to what is
sometimes referred to as the materiality of paint? Is the crust that
Witkin constructs akin to paint qua paint? I think not. In Vermeer's
painting *The Lacemaker* (1669–1670) there is a famous patch where
the skeins of different-colored threads almost dissolve into pure paint,
disconnected from the subject matter of the picture. This materiality
of the paint interferes with the wholeness of the painting; a gap opens
up in the picture. That shows us something of the intrication of real,
imaginary, and symbolic in representation. It is a question of the free-
ing up of space. We can think of this as the everyday reality of the
symbolic/imaginary having too much of an upper hand, and the gap

as a breathing space in which the viewer has a moment of freedom from that reality.

In contrast, the space of Witkin's pictures is a sealed space. Everyday reality is usurped by Witkin's reality, the space of womb and tomb. We can think of this as *jouissance* having too much the upper hand and the photographic skin as limiting and organizing its domain. But just as the gap in the Vermeer does not do away with everyday reality, so the photographic skin does not banish *jouissance* from Witkin's picture. Here, too, the picture lets us experience something of the way in which the three registers are knotted together. But it is a different kind of knotting.

The images in Witkin's work are not structured like the images we are familiar with. Our familiar images are structured by the imaginary and the symbolic of the mirror stage. The Other is in the picture; there is the three-dimensional space of the subject and there is sense. Witkin's images, on the other hand, are forged within the psychic space that he constructs and are subordinate to such space. The image thus becomes unfamiliar. This is consonant with the fact that he is not supplementing the disturbance at the level of the image of his body, but rather of the ego. He finds his measure of existence through the ego. And *jouissance* becomes bearable for him.

BARTHES AND WITKIN

Before developing the question of the real ego, I will consider Roland Barthes' (1980) characterization of the photograph in *Camera Lucida* and argue that Witkin's photographs just do not fit the description. Juli Carson (this volume) has argued that the critic of *Camera Lucida* has done a psychoanalytic job on his own relation to the photograph. Barthes resolves his anxiety at his inability to find the essence of his dead mother in any number of photographs through a move that is to be understood analytically.

The anxiety is produced through what Barthes sees as the fundamental parallel between the photograph and the subject. Such a parallel is based on some shared paradoxes. The photograph and the subject can each be characterized by a certain loss. For there is no pure photographic indexicality unmediated by language, just as there is no subject outside language. There is also a temporal aspect of this loss for both photograph and subject. Barthes emphasizes the paradox of the then-there quality of the photograph that exists simultaneously with its here-now quality. The similarity of the structure of photograph and subject sparks the viewer's identification with the photograph. Carson's argument is that the anxiety that the paradoxes give rise to, in relation to the quest for the essence of the dead mother, abates only with Barthes' analysis of the Winter Garden photograph of her as a girl. This comes about through the punctum. In Barthes' changing view of the punctum, it is at first that which "pricks" the picture and agitates the paradoxes and many different features may serve as the *punctum*; but finally Barthes locates it in the temporal paradox that all photographs present.

This is how Carson describes his search for the *punctum* that finally yields the essence of his mother:

> . . . then finally, amid the images at hand, he "finds" her . . . "the moment that everything turned around," when "he discovered her *as into herself*." And it is at this moment that the mother, whom he had nursed on her deathbed in a primordial return to the original dyad, becomes *his* little girl. . . . The "truth" of the punctum, after all, was *not* in the singular detail but in the stunning reversal of temporal roles, the moment in which the drive's contrary impulse toward life and death displays itself along the atemporal vectors of a moebius strip. [p. 91, this volume]

I think that this traversal of the surface of a moebius strip is a moment when the two sides of the temporal paradox give way and time no longer exists. It is a moment of return to the original dyad. It is a moment, to use the terminology of Seminar XI, when the satisfaction of the drive is achieved by the tracing of a path around the object *a*. Carson's analysis separates Barthes from the paradox of temporal loss and makes good the loss of his mother. He no longer identifies with the photograph and its loss.

Barthes' sublimatory move could not be further from the way in which Witkin deals with the paradoxes of temporality and loss. In his pictures time exists as eternity and loss is turned into presence. Then and there is the same time and place as here and now. There is no loss; the indexicality of the photograph and the presence of the subject are fully realized. Barthes *starts* with a relation of identification with the photograph and then distances himself from it in a moment of sublimatory satisfaction. Witkin *ends* by turning himself into a photograph, not in an identificatory moment with the Barthesian paradoxes, but in a bizarre personal solution to his problems of *jouissance*, by bolting himself into place. I find that I have spoken of movement in relation to Barthes and of being bolted into place in relation to Witkin. The first distances himself from the photograph; the second locks himself into the photograph. There is sublimation in the one case, and painful *jouissance* in the other.

I can show you this more clearly in relation to the role of life and death in the two cases. The Winter Garden photograph concerns the paradox of life and death (both the photograph and the subject). And for Barthes (1984), as we have seen, the two sides of the paradox are transcended at the moment of reversal in his response to the Winter Garden photograph, the moment his mother becomes *his* little girl. He writes: "During her illness, I nursed her, held the bowl of tea she liked because it was easier to drink from than a cup; she had become my little girl, uniting for me with that essential child she was in her first photograph" (p. 72).

A few lines further on he explains how this reversal changes his relation to Life and Death:

> Ultimately I experienced her, strong as she had been, my inner law, as my feminine child. Which was my way of resolving Death. If . . . Death is the harsh victory of the race, if the particular dies for the satisfaction of the universal, if after having been reproduced as other than himself, the individual dies, having thereby denied and transcended himself, I who had not procreated, I had, in her very illness, engendered my mother. Once she was dead I no longer had any reason to attune myself to the progress of the superior

> Life Force (the race, the species). My particularity could never
> again universalise itself (unless . . . by writing, whose project hence-
> forth would become the unique goal of my life). [p. 72]

The distinction that is transcended or resolved in Barthes is collapsed
and congealed in Witkin. With the latter there is no distinction between life and death, just as there is no distinction between past and
present. The fundamental difference between the two men is that
Witkin makes no attempt to distance himself from the photograph;
there is nothing like the movement of reversal we find in Barthes. This
lack of movement dismantles the operation of the drive.

Barthes knew this. A final quotation on the difference between
cinema and photography makes this clear:

> . . . the cinema has a power which at a first glance the Photograph
> does not have: the screen . . . is not a frame but a hideout; the man
> or woman who emerges from it continues living: a "blind field"
> constantly doubles our partial vision. Now, confronting millions
> of photographs, including those which have a good *studium*, I sense
> no blind field: everything which happens within the frame dies
> absolutely once this frame is passed beyond. When we define the
> Photograph as a motionless image, this does not mean only that
> the figures it represents do not move; it means that they do not
> *emerge*, do not *leave*: they are anesthetised and fastened down, like
> butterflies. Yet once there is a *punctum*, a blind field is created.
> [pp. 55–57]

Witkin has got rid of the *punctum*. There is then zero distance between
him and the photograph. Not only does he refuse the sublimatory
move, he is not content even to remain at the level of the paradoxes
of the photograph and the identification with it. He must turn himself into a photograph.

JOYCE AND WITKIN: INTEGUMENT AND SKIN

This returns us to the question of how the work can build the real
ego of the artist. What does it mean to turn yourself into a book and

a photograph? For both Witkin and Joyce, the construction of the ego concerns making marks. Let's look first at Joyce. The marks that Joyce makes make reference to language. At the same time they obliterate meaning. We can see this taking shape in *A Portrait of the Artist as a Young Man*. Stephen, the stand-in for Joyce, on the occasion when his father seeks his name on the old college desks at Queen's, sees the word "foetus" cut several times into the dark, stained wood. Onto this word he superimposes others. The names he repeats to himself are the effort to pin down the "foetus," to keep it in place. But the repetition of names is not enough. As Lacan says, it is through écriture, a writing in the real, that Joyce solves the problem of how to pin down the real. A passage from *Finnegans Wake* (1939) is most revealing here.[52]

> Then, pious Eneas, conformant to the fulminant firman which enjoins on the tremylose terrian that, when the call comes, he shall produce nichthemerically from his unheavenly body a no uncertain quantity of obscene matter not protected by copriright in the United States of Ourania or bedeed and bedood and bedang and bedung to him, with this double dye, brought to blood heat, gallic acid on iron ore, through the bowels of his misery, flashly, faithly, nastily, appropriately, this Esuan Menschavik and the first till last alshemist wrote over every square inch of the only foolscap available, his own body, till by its corrosive sublimation one continuous present tense integument slowly unfolded all marryvoising, moodmoulded cyclewheeling history. [pp. 185–186]

What is this, if not an account of the real ego? The idea of a "continuous present tense integument" identifies the page as the "foolscap" of Joyce's own body. His writing forms this skin/rind of his body. At the same time, this is not a body ego. Certainly the body and the skin/rind are rendered inseparable but only because, simultaneously, body and foolscap are also inseparable. I am not aware that Lacan used this particular passage from Joyce when he said that Joyce made himself into a book, but that thought is unmistakably here in Joyce.

---

52. I am grateful to Luke Thurston for drawing this passage to my attention.

Witkin, similarly, constructs an ego by making marks and makes himself into a picture. The skin of Witkin's pictures is at the same time the skin of Witkin's body. He makes marks on the photographic negative and on the print to pin down the real and allow himself to exist. But this is at the cost of the representational space of the Other. We could say that Witkin disrupts vision. The Witkinian ego is constructed at the cost of seeing.

SHITTING WITH IMPUNITY

What does the making of marks in the making of the real ego mean? I suggest that this making is shitting. The theme is there in Joyce: "he shall produce nichthemerically from his unheavenly body a no uncertain quantity of obscene matter not protected by copriright. . . ." Joyce and Witkin shit and shit. But don't all artists work with shit? Pictures may well be made *of* shit, but Witkin transforms pictures *into* shit. The skin of the picture is this shit, and so also is the skin/ego/picture of Witkin himself.

I think that this gives us a clue as to why Witkin comes to have some existence through his work. It has to do with the role of shit in the constitution of the subject. Lacan discusses this in his unpublished Seminar X, *L'Angoisse* (1963–1964, Session of August 28, 1963), which concerns itself with the forms of the object *a*. He says that at the oral stage the subject cannot know the degree to which he is himself the being stuck on the breast of his mother, in the form of the nipple. In contrast, in the anal stage, he recognizes himself in the object that he can hold onto or give up. Of course, this shit is both him and something that must not be him—he mustn't smear with it. The excrement is simultaneously something that is him and must not be him. Now this anal object is the cause of anal desire not simply as pure excrement, but as excrement that is demanded by the Other. The object comes to be situated where demand dominates and shit is valorized as it gives satisfaction to the demand of the Other.

I suggest that when Witkin and Joyce shit and shit, they function in an old mode of subjectification. But this time it is not literally a question of excrement and it has nothing to do with the satisfaction of the Other. With Witkin and Joyce it is not so much a question of anal desire as of an inert once-valorized object. All we can say is that the "regression" concerns an identification with the object. We have to suppose that an unfamiliar economy is in place wherein the "regression" to the anal subverts its usual effects—now it becomes a way of freezing desire and remaining outside the demand of the Other.

REFERENCES

Barthes, R. (1980). *Camera Lucida*. London: Fontana, 1984.

Celant, G. (1995). *Witkin*. Milan: Scalo.

Joyce, J. (1916). *A Portrait of the Artist as a Young Man*. In *The Essential James Joyce*, ed. H. Levin, pp. 51–252. Harmondsworth, UK: Penguin, 1963.

———— (1937). *Ulysses*. London: The Bodley Head.

———— (1939). *Finnegans Wake*. Harmondsworth, UK: Penguin, 1992.

Parry, E. (1998). Convalescent . . . incorruptible. In *The Bone House: Joel-Peter Witkin*. Santa Fe, NM: Twin Palm Publishers.

Thurston, L. (1998). *Writing the Symptom: Lacan's Joycean Knot*. Doctoral thesis, University of Kent, Canterbury, UK. Unpublished.

Witkin, J.-P. (1987). The grotesque as the elevation of the self. In *Repulsion: Aesthetics of the Grotesque*, curator A. I. Ludwig. New York: The Alternative Museum.

Index